HENRY EDWARD WILBY'S REMARKABLE JOURNEY

AROUND CAPE HORN FROM PORTUGAL TO SAN FRANCISCO

14 Jan 1850 - 17 Oct 1851

Henry Edward Wilby
as a young man

MAGDALENA GORRELL GUIMARAENS

Library of Congress Control Number: 2021945788

ISBN   Paperback   978-1-68536-011-5
              eBook   978-1-68536-012-2

Westwood Books Publishing LLC
Atlanta Financial Center
3343 Peachtree Rd NE Ste 145-725
Atlanta, GA 30326

www.westwoodbookspublishing.com

CONTENTS

PART 1

FORWARD

This is the story of Henry Edward Wilby, the son of a prominent 19th-century British Merchant of Porto, Portugal, who with two friends purchased a sailing vessel in 1849 and set off on an intrepid voyage around the tip of South America to supply California gold miners with staple goods.

In choosing to load a ship with goods, to travel to a new land to trade them and explore a new commercial venture, Henry Edward and his friends were continuing the tradition of the British traders who had traveled to Portugal since the end of the 17th century. Most of these were the sons or factors of English and Scottish general merchants who had traded cloth and cotton thread with Portugal since the 14th and 15th centuries, in exchange for a range of local commodities they shipped to London, Bristol, Liverpool and Hull, namely wine, raw wool, salt, cork, honey, fruit and codfish.

*   *   *

British northerners in Porto, mainly Yorkshiremen but also Scots and Lancastrians, were notable in numerous fields on which the early Porto British Community depended: John Carr of York, architect of the Santo Antonio Hospital, John Whitehead, architect of the Factory House and Consul, general merchants, shipping agents, early chaplains and schoolmasters. The names of these men and their families are all familiar in the commercial history of the city: Atkinson, Whitely, Rawes, Sellers, Laidley, Flower, Wilby, Gordon, Pye and Cassels, to name but a few.

* * *

This story is based on my extensive research into the genealogy and history of the Wilby and Guimaraens families, on Henry Edward Wilby's personal diaries and exerpts from the *Bella Pernambucana*'s ship's log, made available to me by John Wilby for purposes of a first family reunion in Vancouver, entries in the Guimaraens Family Bible and contributions from Wilby descendants in Canada, England, Portugal and Australia.

The diaries, hand-written by Henry Edward, can be divided into three time periods. The first actually begins, as he and his partners approach the Southernmost tip of South America after they had been almost 3 months at sea. The second period, as they land in Valparaiso, Chile, and the third and last, with their arrival in San Francisco. Henry Edward pens descriptions of when they dock and begin trading, relations between the partners, the several devastating fires that frequently swept the city, the deaths of fellow seamen by drowning and several public hangings of criminals.

In transcribing the text of the diaries I corrected the spelling of certain Portuguese names and place names for accuracy, translating some for greater ease of understanding. For the same reason, I took the liberty of using a uniform dating for the entries and adding the occasional punctuation mark. I have also annotated several entries with information that has since come to light from news reports of the period and my research. These notes and annotations appear as footnotes.

My special thanks to Dianne Levy, webmaster of The Maritime Heritage Project, who was most helpful in finding further information on Henry Edward Wilby's ship, the *Bella Pernambucana*, which she informs me was also known as the *Procranna, Procrenna, Procreana,* and other spellings, and in explaining the kind of ships that sailed around the horn at the time.

I am indebted to websites such as the one for the San Francisco Museum and the several California genealogy sites from which I was able to obtain a lot of information regarding the goldrush times. I have referenced these source wherever appropriate.

Magdalena Gorrell Guimaraens
Vila Nova de Cerveira, Portugal, 2021

PART 2

THE WILBY FAMILY OF YORKSHIRE AND PORTUGAL

The well-known Wilby family of British Merchants went to Porto, Portugal, from Dewsbury, Yorkshire, in the North of England, where they were well-established clothiers and wool merchants. Henry Edward, the hero of this adventure, was the first of this family to be born in Portugal. His grandfather, Jonathan Wilby, was a wealthy merchant of considerable standing in Yorkshire, who was born and bred in Hartshead, near Dewsbury, where he lived and died. The Wilby family Bible indicates that Henry Edward's parents, William and Ann, were probably married by Patrick Brontë from Haworth, as he was also serving as curate in St. Peter's, Hartshead, at the time.

Wilby family ties to Porto and Lisbon

Jonathan and Mary (Dyson) Wilby had eight children but it was four of their grandchildren who were to provide the family's first direct links to Portugal: grandaughter Mary married Thomas Chaster, agent for the Bible Society in Lisbon; grandson William was an established Merchant of Porto, his brother John was a merchant member of the British Factory in Lisbon, and their sister Mary Elizabeth married James Rawes of Borrowdale in Cumbria, a general merchant and shipping agent who came to Porto where he entered into partnership with William A. Tait whose first wife, Dorothy Maria, was Thomas Chaster's sister.

When William's son Henry Edward married Eliza Antoinette Searle, the Wilbys became related to the Laidley and Flower families of Porto and Lisbon and to the Searles of Figueira da Foz, Madeira and Chile. As we shall see, these relationships played a major role in the California venture.

William Wilby, Henry Edward's father

William Wilby, Henry Edward's father, was born in Hartshead, Yorkshire, in 1799. We do not know exactly when he came to Porto, although his daughter Sarah Alice Gordon believed it was around 1820 when he was 21 years of age. He was a general merchant who imported woolen and cotton cloth from Yorkshire and exported raw wool, wine and other goods from Porto. He is also believed to have imported the first Yorkshire White breed of pigs that are so popular in Portugal today.

A leading and active member of the community, in 1825 William was a signatory to a petition to the Secretary of State for Foreign Affairs in London, complaining about the Consul's behaviour in barring general merchants from the Factory House in Porto. A hard-headed, outspoken Yorkshireman and staunch Liberal, family tradition has it that William provided the inspiration for Richard Whitestone, the principle character in his friend Julio Dinis' book *A Família Inglesa*, a Portuguese literary classic.

* * *

During a visit home to Yorkshire, William married his cousin Ann and the couple built their home in Caldas de Vizela, in the heart of the Portuguese textile industry, in the north of the country. A 19th-century photograph by Frederick Flower shows William's house, on the hillside above the Roman bridge, a short walk from the derelict Roman baths that William helped restore in later years. William was extremely well-liked in Vizela where he is still remembered as *O Senhor do Chalet*.

Vizela, similar in size and geography to Dewsbury in Yorkshire, was a thriving mill town, so it is no surprise that William made this his primary home and that he played a key role in introducing many of the innovations that Yorkshire manufacturers were pioneering as part of the industrial revolution that was sweeping the textile trade in England, particularly mechanization of the spinning mills by harnessing of the water power of the river.

*   *   *

William Wilby also owned a house in Porto, on the Rua de São Cosmé, overlooking the River Douro, to which he moved his young family during the turbulent years that preceeded the Liberal Revolution and Siege of Porto (1832-1834) and it was here that Henry Edward was born on May 4, 1823. His sister was born here in March 1830. As Ann Wilby became desperately ill after the birth of her daughter, William decided to take his wife and baby back to her family in Yorkshire.

After burying all the family silver and other valuables in the Vizela gardens for safekeeping and leaving 7-year-old Henry in Vizela, in the care of a governess and his faithful manservant until their return, William obtained a safe-conduct pass to Lisbon where he, his wife and baby daughter embarked on a ship to England. Sadly, Ann died soon after their arrival in Hartshead. Before returning to Porto in 1835, once the siege of Porto was over and the political situation had settled, William married, a second time, Sarah Ann Biglands from Wigton in Cumberland.

Henry Edward Wilby

Henry Edward acquired five stepsisters from his father's second marriage, four of whom were born in Porto: Leonora Elivira, a gifted artist who never married and lived for some time in Paris, where she died and is buried; Sarah Alice, who married George Gordon, a young man from Bolton in Lancashire who came to Porto to build a spinning mill in Crestuma, near Porto, and remained as Manager;

Mary Reis, who died as a child; and Louisa Georgiana, who never married. His youngest sister, Wilhelmina Elizabeth was born in Wigton, Cumberland, but she died a year later in Vizela whilst Henry Edward was sailing to California. Henry Edward's niece, Grace Haigh Gordon, married Manoel Pedro Guimaraens of Fonseca Port; her brother, Frank Biglands Gordon, was employed by another Port Wine shipper, Robertson Brothers.

Henry Edward's sister Lavinia married Doctor Ricardo Gomes da Costa, physician to the Portuguese Royal Family in Porto and they had one son. When William Wilby died in Porto in 1881, in his 83rd year, he had a total of 16 grandchildren - 9 from his first marriage and 7 from his second.

* * *

Nothing is known of Henry Edward's whereabouts during the five years that his father remained in Yorkshire, but it is possible that at some point he returned to Hartshead as, in an interview published in the Vancouver Press, his widow stated that he had gone to school in Yorkshire before training in commercial matters with the Laidley firm in Lisbon. He was also employed for a time by the Portuguese government to superintend some road building in the North of the country. In 1884, Henry Edward sold the family home in Vizela to provide an income for his widowed mother and his unmarried sister Louisa Georgiana. A cottage next to the bridge and belonging to the property was retained by the extended family as a weekend and holiday retreat for many years.

PART 3

THE ADVENTURE BEGINS

When in April 1848 a West Coast newspaper published the first rumours that gold had been discovered in the territory of California, the city of San Francisco, a gloomy town with few commercial prospects, had a population of only four hundred and sixty persons. Within a month, as the immense wealth in the gold fields became apparent, nearly everyone had gone off to the mines and the town had become substantially deserted. In May, the newspaper complained:

> "The whole country from San Francisco to Los Angeles, and from the sea shore to the base of the Sierra Nevadas, resounds with the sordid cry of gold, GOLD, GOLD! while the field is left half planted, the house half built, and everything is neglected but the manufacture of shovels and pickaxes."

The newspaper closed for want of staff, shops were abandoned, food production ceased and there was a serious risk of famine in the region as local inhabitants fled to the mines and thousands of adventurers made their way to the city. In the autumn, vessels from every direction, laden with provisions, clothing and all kinds of saleable goods, converged on San Francisco, the nearest port to the gold fields.

By the Spring of 1849, the population of the city had risen to over 50,000 persons. As the harbour filled with ships, barques and schooners, many of the old residents who saw a better chance of making money in trade and speculation than by digging for gold, returned to the city and many others followed. Business revived, there was ample employment at high wages, real estate rose in value and the town, which a few months before had been nearly deserted, boomed with a progress that reads almost like a fairy tale, with a population of one hundred thousand.

Searle, Wilby & Clark and the *Bella Pernambucana*

Henry Edward's decision to sail to California was no doubt prompted by the fact that two close friends of his were already there. Anthony Van Dam Searle's eldest son, James sailed to California on his own ship in early 1849 and met up with Henry Laidley from Lisbon. That May, James' brother John Searle, was appointed Portuguese Consul in San Francisco. As other members of the Searle family were successful merchants in Madeira and Chile, I suspect that it was William Wilby's considered opinion that supplying goods and merchandise to the gold miners in San Francisco could be a wise commercial decision, particularly if both families were united in such a venture. Accordingly, Henry Edward formed a partnership with his close friend John Searle and Joseph Clark, another young Englishman.

Trading under the name of Searle, Wilby & Clark, the three young men purchased a three-masted barque, the *Bella Pernambucana*, filled it with goods for sale and on consignment and prepared to sail for California under the Portuguese flag. Although John Searle was nominally the senior partner and captain, it was Henry Edward who financed the largest share of the venture from his savings and subsequent loans from his father and his uncle John Wilby in Lisbon, as the need arose.

An experienced British seaman, John Bannister, was engaged as Captain and navigator; the cook was black and the rest of the crew was Portuguese.

Captain John Bannister

By Monday, 8 October 1849, the ship was fully laden with cargo, the passengers and most of the crew were on board, the last preparations were being made for the voyage and William Wilby sent a present of three dozen cases of old wine for the journey. The weather, however, was terrible: it was raining heavily, there was a strong westerley wind, a very strong current in the river and the bar of the River Douro was closed to all shipping. John Searle and his brother George, who would marry Fanny Flower and who had come up from Figueira to see them off, slept on board; Henry Edward stayed off and on at his father's home in Porto.

As the days passed, John and Henry Edward's tempers became increasingly frayed: they were operating on a very tight budget and every extra day they lost cost them money they could ill afford. Henry Edward's diary for this period swings from details of the difficulties in obtaining more money from his father to cover these additional expenses, to his feelings for his fiancée, Eliza Searle, to whom he had become engaged. Eliza was George and John Searle's sister and a close friend of John's fiancée, Sophia Laidley.

Henry Edward's main problem was that he was torn between his impatience at setting sail and spending every free moment he could manage with Eliza whom he would meet at the Tait house, under the watchful eye of Mrs. William A. Tait, his uncle Thomas Chaster's sister Dorothy. Finally, on Sunday the 21st, he spent his last evening with Eliza alone:

"We remained in the dining room as these few hours of my Liz's company is too precious to be lost. At parting, Liz tied a scarf of hers about my neck and again we parted with a smile, for the last time! Though we did not then know for certain that it was so. I then called at home and we went all together on board - John, Captain Bannister, Clark and I. A little after one o'clock in the morning, we were all awoke by a Pilot hailing us from the quay, with orders from the *Piloto Mor* to take charge of the *Bella Pernambucana* and be ready to sail by daylight. In a few minutes the Pilot came on board and all was prepared for sailing. I dressed and ran up to town to call my Father and George, who accompanied me on board.

As soon as it was light the ship was got underway. George and my Father left us near the bar and at 6 o'clock we crossed the bar in safety, along with several other vessels. Here we are at last on the open sea, in our good old Bark *Bella Pernambucana*.

The occupants of our cabin are, our three selves (that is myself and partners), Captain Bannister (our navigator), Gregorio da Piedade (our mate and boatswain), Senhor Morães (a passenger for Rio de Janeiro), Senhor Leão (ditto) and our two servants (José Maria Cavalleiro and Antonio Dias) and Jonathan, Roberto's son and servant, and in the half deck, one passenger for Rio. I was sick most of the day although the sea was quite smooth with scarcely any wind."

Four days later, after some slow sailing due to the lack of wind, our adventurers finally arrived in Lisbon where they had to put the ship's papers in order before they could sail further - the Harbour Authority in Porto had neglected to specify the number of passengers and crew in the ship's Bill of Health and because of this they were almost put in quarantine.

Putting the papers in order and the enforced stay of several more days cost them even more money, which Henry Edward, much to his annoyance, had to borrow from his Uncle John as neither Searle nor Clark had brought any with them. Finally, they were off on their way to Rio.

THE ROUTE

The wooden three-masted barque was a common sight in the port of San Francisco in the middle of the 19th century. Until the fast, elegant clippers and huge steamers began arriving in 1850-1851, barques, ships and brigs carried huge cargo loads from around the world. The route of the Windjammers and steamships joining the Pacific ports of the US with her Atlantic ports and Europe required rounding Cape Horn. This was the only maritime route passing the Americas prior to the opening of the Panama Canal.

In: Allan Villiers, National Geographic Magazine, 1931

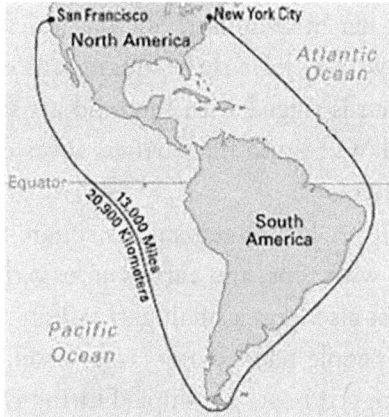

Cape Horn

Cape Horn is one of the stormiest and most dangerous passages in the world. Winds blow cold and constant between 35 - 125 knots. Waves are between 80 to 120 feet rising out of freezing cold water and the likelihood of survival once overboard is minimal.

Cape Horn is the steep headland on Horn Island, part of Tierra del Fuego, in southern Chile. It is the southernmost point of South

America and extends into Drake Passage. The cape was sighted by Sir Francis Drake in 1578, but it was named for the birthplace (Hoorn) of the Dutch navigator Willem Schouten, who first sailed around it in 1616. The Strait of Magellan, discovered in 1520 by Ferdinand Magellan and the preferred route ever since, lies to the north.

❧❧❧

Ships

Barque (or Bark) A barque is square-rigged at fore and main masts, and differs from a ship in having no top, and carrying only fore-and-aft sails at her mizzenmast. She has at least three masts. All of them are rigged with at least three square sails each, except for the sternmost one, which is rigged with fore-and-aft sails. It is presumed that Henry Edward Wilby and his partners invested in a similar-type ship or small schooner.

Full-rigged ship: A full-rigged ship is square-rigged throughout: she has three masts with tops, and carries at least three square sails on all three masts. Most also have a small gaff sail on the sternmost mast. Even though most people refer to any large vessel as a "ship," strictly speaking only full-rigged boats are ships. During the latter part of the 19th Century, many ships were converted to four-masted barques.

Some of the following information was downloaded from The Maritime Heritage Project website and should prove useful in better understanding the Diary. The webmaster, Dianne Levy, has been most helpful and is attempting to find further information on Henry Edward Wilby's ship, the *Bella Pernambucana*, which she informed me was also known as the *Procranna, Procrenna, Procreana,* and other spellings.

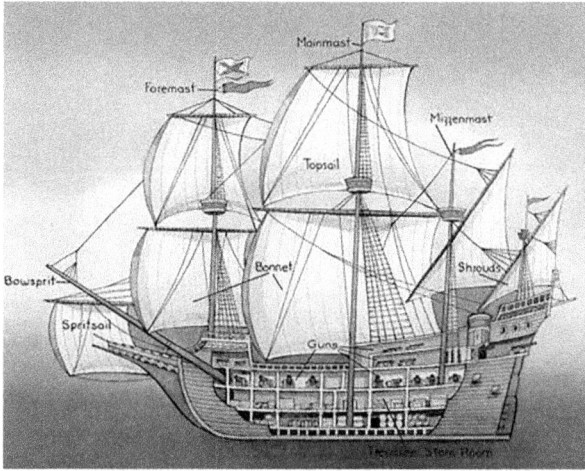

THE SQUARE SAILS	
(a) The Fore Sail	(k) The Main Top-gallant Sail
(b) The Fore Topsail	(l) The Main Top-gallant Royal
(c) The Fore Top-gallant Sail	(m) The Main Topmast Studding Sail
(d) The Fore Top-gallant Royal	(n) The Main Top-gallant Studding Sail
(e) The Fore Studding Sail	(o) The Mizen Topsail
(f) The Fore Topmast Studding Sail	(p) The Mizen Top-gallant Sail
(g) The Fore Top-gallant Studding Sail	(q) The Mizen Top-gallant Royal
(h) The Mainsail	(r) The Spritsail
(i) The Main Topsail	(s) The Spritsail Topsail

THE FORE AND AFT SAILS	
The Jib	The Main Top-gallant Staysail
The Fore Topmast Staysail	The Mizen Staysail
The Fore Staysail	The Mizen Topmast Sail
The Main Staysail	The Mizen Top-gallant Staysail
The Main Topmast Staysail	The Driver or Spanker and
The Middle Staysail	the Mizen brailed up

PART 4

THE DIARY

Monday, 14 January 1850

At 10:30 to 11:00 last, was awoke by much noise on deck, the water swishing by her sides at a great rate warned me there was a stiff breeze. And hearing all busy shortening sail, dressed. The scene was awfully grand, the sea curling around us in angry form, whilst the old ship dashed over it in gallant style. She must have been going at 11 to 12 knots. She had much canvas on her and it appeared to lift her out of the water. It rained a little but we were all soon hard at work shortening sail. The lower sansail was carried away and with difficulty we got in the sail. Royals, all light double reefed, main topsail and whilst others were doing their best to triple reef the fore topsail, the wind split it in pieces and with difficulty we got the men all safe on deck. John[1] who had been at the wheel ran to help and left me in his place. She was now laying to only with the close reefed main to sail, which she did easily.

At 12 o'clock on the night of 13th to 14th of the month, I at wheel in a storm, could I have exchanged that place for another …at same day of month, same time past! I was pensive though not frightened. Poor Laidley was in a great funk. The staysail was set, but the storm split it and towards morning the mizzen set and also split; at last the

---

[1] John Searle.

fury of the storm abated a little and before daylight I turned in. Up at 8:00, mainsail and foresail set with new fore topgallant sail close reefed. About midday the storm abated a little and we shook the reefs out. At night it came almost calm with a great sea. Ship rolling much. Yankee whale ship passed us on another tack, close under our lee, showed our flag. In the night rudder chains parted.

Tuesday, 15ᵗʰ January

Becalmed in a heavy sea. Plenty of birds astern, caught one with hook and line, black hooked bill, a little white about the head, size of a duck. Mate confined to his bed with rheumatism. Bannister[2] keeps watch in his place. Killed a pig.

13ᵗʰ January, the storm commenced at 6:00 and by ten had to lay to till Tuesday morning when it settled down, but left a heavy sea and calm. First storm.

Wednesday, 16ᵗʰ January

Very little wind and that ahead, albatrosses in sight. Clark, Laidley and I shot one down and brought it on board. It measures 9 ½ feet from tip of wings. I stuffed the bird caught by the lines with sand.

Thursday, 17ᵗʰ January

Calm, more albatrosses under our stern. Searle shot one with a ball from his little gun, I went in the gig to fetch it and whilst on my way a bird like the one I stuffed, wheeled round me and I shot it and had no sooner reloaded than I shot an albatross. Brought down dead. It was as large as any of the others; brought all three birds on board, the sailors cooked them and all ate of them but me. I could not for the stink they emitted in skinning. Searle skinned the feet and the skin made nice little bags. Busy making main sail.

---

[2] John Bannister, Captain of the *Bella Pernambucana*

Friday, 18th January

Stiff breeze but against her, taught bowline all day; all agreed very well from Rio here and boatswain keeps the men in order; towards evening a heavy sea. (Evening tic douloureux[3])

Saturday, 19th January

Becalmed nearly all day with a very heavy sea, enough to toss the masts out of her, such indeed as to come over the bows of our quarter boats.

Sunday, 20th January

Gentle breeze died to calm at 8 and at 12 freshened again a little. Heavy swell. A whale seen in the morning watch. Sermon.

Monday, 21st January – 2nd storm

Morning fine, clothes out to dry, hard work splicing stunsail boom. Towards evening, lightening astern, stiff breeze astern. All sails set, but about 6 p.m., being jealous of the looks of the weather, furled all light sails. Mate's barometer useless. Mate who has been bedridden for a week with rheumatism was up today; at 7:00 breeze freshened to a storm and blew with awful fury and before we got the foresail furled the wind split it in several pieces; our men were afraid to trust themselves on the yard for it bent like a reed.

*   *   *

Bannister mounted the shrouds first; the black cook (whose intrepidity is deserving of notice) followed him along with eight men and boys. Bannister got the starboard side of the sailed furled, but those on the larboard funked [*sic.*] and came down. Bannister and his few went over and furled it. Now came two tough jobs to do. To reef

---

3   *Trigeminal neuralgia.* Painful, involuntary twitching of the facial muscles, sometimes unilateral. SYN., *Bell's spasm.*

the two topsails. After much work we got them both triple reefed. We then came below, unable to bear the wet and cold. Bannister at 9, came down and said to Searle: "Jump up, we must lay to, the wind is too furious to sail any longer".

Up we went and furled all up but the triple reefed mizzen topsail and she came to it beautifully; the mizzen began to shake loose and seven men went to furl it but such was the fury of the gale, that it took better than half an hour to do. The boatswain had to go up to it also or it would have gone away when all were on it. They called out to haul on the clue-lines which I tried to do, but drew about a foot and to hold that I had the blood started at my finger ends. But had I let go, away had gone the sail; my call for help could not be heard though but a few yards from me were several persons. I succeeded in belaying it.

*   *   *

Soon after a cry rose of man overboard. I let go of the weather rigging and slid to leeward along with John where João the *Moro*[4] was laid half in the quarter boat and half overboard. I pulled him in and took him below. He had fallen from the top of the mizzen, but not much hurt. Had he gone over he must inevitably have been lost. Soon after, Manuel *Gallego*[5] fell also off the mizzen and sprained his foot. Brought him down almost scared to death. Soon after the mizzen got furled and the boys were allowed to come in the cabin; we got them clothes to change and allowed them to sit in here.

*   *   *

The wind continued to increase and we to tremble for our main topsail, and to wish we had the new one bent. But we were cold and tired

---

[4] Portuguese for John the Arab; he probably was very dark-skinned.

[5] Manuel, from Galicia in Northern Spain. Many *gallegos* came from this very poor region to find work.

and took two or three snatches of sleep, though but for a few minutes. Our sails kept getting unfurled, such was the fury of [the] storm, and hard work it was to lash them again. Launch loose. Staysail up.

Tuesday, 22nd January

Three months today since we left Porto and we are in a storm such as none on board ever saw, its fury increases instead of lessening, the men completely exhausted and so it continued all day; no cooking, men had raw [*sic.* meat and] water. From 8 to 9 the main topsail on which our hopes rested broke loose, the iron hooks parted from the chain sheets and the ship flew up and shipped a tremendous sea over the quarter, covering Searle, Captain, Mate and boatswain and Antonio. I was in my bed when in it flew by the cabin door and under my bed, coming just up to my mattress. I laid still and bailed it out into the cabin whence Antonio baled it out with buckets, Laidley sadly frightened [*sic.*]. Meanwhile they caught the beck of the sail and got it fast and set up again and up came the ship. Soon after the staysail (fore topmast) was all but gone and several seas shipped carrying away the larboard bulwarks. The boatswain and crew went forward and offered up to *Sra. da Bonança*[6] for their safety, they then took courage whilst they were thus employed.

* * *

I had fastened the cabin doors leaving only the top part open, then going to my room offered up my prayers for safety and came out on deck. (Clark ironically said we are in a nasty storm, perhaps a capful of prayers would help us; both John and Bannister turned reprovingly to him and said this is no time for useless bravado, we perhaps need them and perhaps we had all been wishing for several hours past that we could forget many things we had done or that they had never been done; imagine Clark's position, abashed his feelings, mine calm and

---

6   Our Lady of Kindness. In other words, they prayed.

sere a proud swelling of the bosom, said to myself: "Yes, the prayers you disdain have been offered to my Father and they will not be in vain. He has heard me, I feel it." Went on deck, silent.

In the course of an hour the fury of the storm abated a little and continued to do so during the night. Searle said this makes one think of those we left behind us. I said it needed not this to remind me of them. At twelve we went again before the wind, under storm canvass and all turned in but Bannister, cold, starved and tired out, not having been able to cook or have fire on board.

Wednesday, 23rd January

Rousted up at 8 to breakfast, ravenous, each a tin can of chocolate and plate of *farinha de pau*[7], nothing else cookable. One of our poor boys, Cazapia, had his breeches blown to atoms in the storm, so I gave him a pair[8] and to Zé Maria who also behaved well, I gave an old short coat. Two ducks in rice and beef for dinner and ate like savages; very cold; plenty of albatross close under the stern, two were caught with hook and line and bit of pork; whale seen. Early to bed tired out. Clothes drying.

Thursday, 24th January

Light winds, small rain, everything damp and uncomfortable. Whale alongside, very large.

Friday, 25th January

Fine dry day, cold. Clark took the Stewardship out of my hands, clothes to dry, I busy with the stunsail boom, finished it. Hooked another albatross. Lots of kelp or seaweed passed us indicating our nearing the Falklands.

---

[7]   Mandioc flour, usually sautéed in a little fat with bits of meat or fish.

[8]   In those days, sailors were so very poor they rarely had a change of clothes, sleeping and working in the same garments.

Saturday, 26ᵗʰ January

Excessive cold, gave away an old coat and trousers to the boys, evening fresh breeze aft. Obliged to take in sail to close reefed topsails and foresail; rolling much during night, going 10 knots.

Sunday, 27ᵗʰ January

Excessive cold, dry and sunny. Put on flannel drawers, shirt and woollen stockings but did not feel much warmer for them. Fair wind aft during the morning. Evening taught bowline. Wind appears determined to thwart our intention of going to the west of the Falkland Islands. Sermon read.

Monday, 28ᵗʰ January

Excessive cold, dry and sun, moderate breeze aft. Obliged to go outside the Falklands, altered course accordingly. In the afternoon four porpoises made their appearance. Bannister struck at but missed one. They have black backs and white bellies. John cut finger and fainted.

Tuesday, 29ᵗʰ January – 3ʳᵈ storm

Rain, stiff breeze aft. At 8 A.M. a large ship crossed our bow at some distance, beating to windward, we supposed her to be homeward bound from the Pacific. Soon after she passed, a bottle went by us but out of reach and the sea was too high to lower a boat for it. We supposed it from her and might contain letters or information.

*   *   *

Midday 28 miles east of Berkeley Sound by reckoning, but hazy, no land visible. Soundings 50 fathoms. Towards evening wind increased and by ten, blew a stiff gale S.W., and we had to lay to under close reefed topsail and main trisel. Storm with rain till daybreak. A sea struck the gig and the brake broke; we got the gig inboard lashed. Shipped several seas in the night. One swept her fore and aft carrying away two water casks and a house built over the galley.

Commenced a letter to Liz[9], dated this day off the Falkland Islands and gave her an account of our voyage from the 5th inst., mentioning when I last wrote up to the 12th, inclusive, then knocked off writing.

Wednesday, 30th January

I kept in bed all night though the storm was awful. I did not dread it. The rest had been up all night and got wet several times. Up at 8 and on deck, sun out, sky clear but the storm unabated, the wind bitter cold, sun warm in sheltered parts of ship, the sea rolling mountains high and its white crests glittering in the sunbeams. Our ship acquitted herself nobly, riding easily to it. Several seas came on board, one mounted the quarterdeck and part came into the cabin, and but for precautions, doors shut, could have set us swimming.

No food cooked till evening but some fried pork which each eat out of his fingers. Evening, water half warm to tea. I had arrowroot and went to bed. At midday, an English brig passed northward. We both shewed our colours and she was soon out of sight with a fair wind, we still laying to. Fore toppan lift broke with men on the bard. Weather topsail sheet.

Thursday, 31st January

Clear day, sun out and warm. Up at 8. Sea rough but wind abated and come round to west. Foresail, mizzen, and staysail added to storm sails and ship going south. Last night so cold I abolished sheets and slept in blankets and a carpet over them and slept well. Had a hearty breakfast, ate some *rebuçados*[10] given me in Porto. English brig passed to leeward northwards, shewed flag and we did the same. Saw three whales.

---

9   Eliza Searle, Henry Edward's fiancée
10 Hard candy.

Friday, 1ˢᵗ February

Clear, sun, warm in our teeth. Wind, southwest, heavy sea, which increased towards evening. At night the wind changed to North, which being fair we made all the sail we would, but during the night it fell off, boxed round. At 4 P.M. a Dutch barque passed northwards under close reefed topsail, double reefed main, double reefed mizzen and a few light sails. We shewed our flag and she likewise shewed hers.

In the evening a row forward. The men refused to come to the help saying they had no food because we gave them *Mandioca*[11]. The boatswain told them if the one whose turn it was did not come, he would fetch him. He, João came directly. The boatswain marked out Antonio the *gageiro*[12] as ringleader and told him he did ill to be so as he would perhaps get a taste of the prison for it.

Saturday, 2ⁿᵈ February

Men have usually had six biscuits each per day, but in consequence of their grumbling, today it was served out by weight, 1 lb. per day which is equal to three biscuits and a half pint of *feijões*[13] each, so they are the losers by grumbling. The wind is again foul though less sea, rained all night. In these latitudes north winds always bring rain. Very cold this morning though during the night it was warmer. After midday sun, but thermometer at 43. Towards evening, the wind came round to northwest, fair for us and all set.

Sunday, 3ʳᵈ February

Cold in morning early but at 8 the sun warmed and by 10 thermometer at 50. Wind still fair, NorthWest, but heavy sea. Four large flocks of ducks passed us; the sailor's directory says they are good eating, but it is too rough to lower a boat. Today I made a plum pudding. In the evening saw a whale.

---

[11] Mandioc flour. I.e., the same as the previously mentioned *farinha de pau*.

[12] (Sic]. *gajeiro*. Lookout man; top watch.

[13] Dried beans.

Monday, 4ᵗʰ February

Beautiful morning, fair wind from the NorthWest, sea smooth, and quite warm. Towards midday a dense fog came on and then the sea rose, wind chopped around to the SouthWest, stiff breeze. We thought we were going to have our weekly gale of wind and had to double reef the topsails and furl the other sails, but at midnight the squall passed off and wind came fair again. Ducks seen and two whales. In the afternoon porpoises were also seen.

Tuesday, 5ᵗʰ February

Before I was up an American whaler (ship) with full cargo homeward bound passed us Northward. We both shewed our flags. Beautiful day, quite warm and pleasant, fair wind all day. At midday we were 13 miles south of Cape Horn and about 130 miles east of it. Rough sea but fine weather, all sails set. Whale seen and cape ducks seen.

Wednesday, 6ᵗʰ February

Southwesterly wind driving us back a little southwards. Dry day, sun out, several flocks of ducks and a whale seen. The coldest day yet felt. Bannister pricked the tail of a porpoise with the harpoon.

Thursday, 7ᵗʰ February

Fair wind but little of it, not so cold as usual, sun out. Towards evening the wind freshened aft but looking rather gloomy and squally. We dared not let the reefs out of our sails, going along at night *a bolina*[14] 7½ to 8 knots, a bird appeared diving alongside. Captain Bannister called it a penguin, it was black with short stumpy wings and kept swimming alongside under water, coming up occasionally to breathe. I went to the main chains and thence threw the chains at it, they hit it and rebounded as though they had struck a cork but the blow though not enough to enter its thick coat of feathers was enough to kill it, and

---

[14] *Navegar à bolina* – to sail near the wind.

it floated astern quite dead. Steward José Maria (Misery) turned away and sent for'ard for a dirty lying thief.

Friday, 8th February

Gloomy with small rain, little wind, precious cold again. António (the *gajeiro grande*[15]) put in the place of the steward who being found with Clark's slippers in his possession was turned forward last night and António elected steward in his place. Wind South altered appearance of water.

Saturday, 9th February

Of Cape Horn, at 4 A.M. make the land on our lee beam and from our dead reckoning concluded it to be [Do-Banize's Islands][16] but afterwards found by taking bearings it was too extensive to be them, and at last made it out to be Cape Horn, bearing North east, distance 12 miles, proving a great set to North east; West about at 8 A.M., stood to the South and at midday about and went North West. Wind moderate, saw a seal near the ship. No sun visible.

Sunday, 10th February

Cold. Stood to Northwest till 5 P.M. when we saw the said Islands, bearing South-SouthWest and the Cape on the other side, bearing NorthEast. At 5, we went about and stood to the South again.

Monday, 11th February

Sky clear and sun out, but cold yet, going South, strong breeze and high seas.

---

[15] The big lookout man.

[16] I could find no island with a name anywhere near this one. Closest to Cape Horn could have been Wollaston Islands although these are between Cape Horn and the mainland. There is the Isla dos Estados (Staten Island) but this is quite large. The islands at Cape Horn, actually, are very, very small compared to the others.

Tuesday, 12th February

Weather squally, going South under easy sail; saw a ship, hoisted our colours and hove to for about half an hour to give her time to catch us. She was coming down from the West so she crossed close under our stern. We hailed her and requested the skipper to report to us which he promised to do. She was a Yankee whaler, the *Nassau* of New Bedford, bound to Rio.

Wednesday, 13th February

Fine weather, but cold wind from N.W. Sea tolerably smooth till near sunset when the weather began to look threatening and the sea to rise; by 8 P.M. had stowed all sails but the 2 topsails which were being reefed and the job which four hands were stowing.

*   *   *

Laidley and I were in the cabin when a cry rose of man overboard. We both ran on deck. The poor fellow had just dropped astern of the ship, shrieking, and swimming; a hen coop was thrown overboard, the ship hove to and the gig launched, but as she had been taken in and stowed on the stern lockers it took some time to get her out. The *contramestre*,[17] António, Miguel, João *grande*[18] jumped in; my heart sank within me for I expected to see them no more, the sea was so high. It was raining, but I stood on the poop with a lantern for those in the boat to steer by. It was so cold I had constantly to change the lamp from hand to hand. The sea and wind kept on increasingly rapidly during the boat's absence so that great fears were entertained for her safety; at last she came back, but unable to find the man. We got boat and men safe on board but with great difficulty.

All hands were called aft and a consultation held as to the probability of saving the man's life by laying to, but all concurred that

---

[17] Boatswain.

[18] I.e., Big John

there was not the slightest hope of it, for if he reached the coop he could not hold on to it with the sea there was on, and even if he could do so he must die of cold before morning; besides this he was heavily clothed and was said to have money, about 200,000 *reis* [*sic.*], about him in a belt. The ship during the night would drift far too leeward of the place where he was lost so there could be no hope of finding him. So we though reluctantly, made sail again under triple reefed topsails and main trisail. We sent for his chest into the cabin. His name was José Maria Garcia. This occurrence cast a gloom over all on board, never to be forgotten.

Thursday, 14th February

Still hove to, heading South, very heavy sea and strong wind, and cold squally all day. The chest belonging to the man we lost was opened in presence of the men and found to contain a few clothes and a guitar. These were with the whole of the things belonging him put up to auction and sold for 14/3400 Portuguese money for account of whom it may concern. The men appeared to care very little about the loss of their comrade, but we feel the loss of a fellow creature by such an awful death.

Friday, 15th February

Still hove to as yesterday, sun out, occasionally squalls come on very heavy with hail showers, very heavy sea. Brig seen away to leeward, hove to.

Saturday, 16th February

Still under the same canvas, gale a little less. Went about at 8 A.M. and are going North. Frequent squalls and hail showers, very cold. Brig seen to leeward same as yesterday. Toward evening, wind lessened, foresail set, at night almost calm.

Sunday, 17ᵗʰ February

Fine day but little wind, fair, very smooth sea. Brig seen some distance ahead. We had all canvas loose but by noon quite calm. During the afternoon fair wind freshened and we going west at 3 to 4 knots. Having these last few days been thrown back in our course, we passed today at 8 P.M. exactly over the same place where we lost the man overboard on the 13ᵗʰ, inst., a singular circumstance. The day was not so cold as usual, sun out and very pleasant.

Monday, 18ᵗʰ February

Smooth sea. Becalmed, beautiful day, busy getting new main sail up, sun out and not cold. A larger ship ahead of us to windward, smooth sea.

Tuesday, 19ᵗʰ February

Smooth sea. Very little wind in morning from the North. Freshened a little toward evening from East. We are going west 3 to 4 knots. Membering have in 5 days made only 30 miles of our course. Fine day, sun out, ship near shewed flags, she American, at night penguins astern. Two BottleNoses or Grampus alongside.[19]

Wednesday, 20ᵗʰ February

Beautiful morning, sea smooth, sun out and not cold, wind South East; we are going west with all rags set, stunsails and all, Yankee astern, also with all sail set; during the night we have been going 4, 5 and 6 knots and the wind holds on, all delighted at the prospect of getting on well our course. At midday, set main Royal which has been down since passing the Falkland Islands. Early in the morning a Brig was seen a long way astern but soon lost sight of. Wind freshened to 6½ to 7 knots towards evening but the Yankee does not gain on us, fine night and we

---

[19] Dolphins.

going west North West. Longitude 70 West, Latitude 57 South from Cadiz[20] and 76.10 from Greenwich.

Thursday, 21st February

Smooth sea. Beautiful day. Yankee ship during night kept full away a point or two and this morning is abeam to leeward with every rag set. Staysails between the masts and all set. We still going nearly west, towards midday becalmed, at 4 P.M. wind sprang up from West north west, we tacked out to West south west from there to West.

The Yankee ship was soon out of sight on the other tack, as Bannister said, going right on for the shore which he makes out distant 120 miles. At dusk a ship was seen in the direction in which she disappeared, but if it was her she must have gone about. Jackals, Penguins astern. Clark got hold of my beard in play *de burro*[21] and pulled part of it out. I could not bear it and in trying to loosen his hold twisted his thumb back.

Friday, 22nd February

Smooth sea. Rained, drizzling all day, tacked at 4 P.M. Very cold and dreary. Clark in a mess with his stewardship; he locked up some sweetmeat in the drawer and the steward seeing him do so thought he was distrusted and immediately resigned his place. Clark was in a quandary, he called the man down. Told him he trusted in him and had not done it on his account and assured him that he was going to give him the key [*sic*.], saying: *"Se eu não vinha para lhe dar a chave, acho lá que eu morro já"*[22] – but the man was not easily satisfied and poor José then said he would have nothing more to do with the stewardship. (A very common way of trying to get out of a scrape). With the first steward, he stood bandying threats (on our rods to Bix[23]); the second

---

20 Port in Southern Spain, near Seville.
21 Literally, an ass; i.e., horsing about.
22 Sic. May I be struck dead if I was not about to give you the key.
23 ?

because he was a poor cursed worm who dared not answer, he bullied and rousted out and turned forward, and to this third one, as he shewes his spirit, we find Clark giving a hundred *satisfações*[24] in vain; at last the man staid in his place, Clark giving him the key.

I would never have subjected myself to such degradation as he did. But the consequence be what it might, but those who by their want of stable sense get themselves into scrapes; the man left and gone forward, Clark would have to do his work for him, for I doubt if any of the others would like to become No. 4 under such a turk.

I felt unwell all day and turned in early. Porpoises came under the bows. Bannister struck one, but it got away. Four months today since we left Porto. Sea rather rough. At midday we were furthest west of all the voyage being longitude 76 from Cadiz or 82¼ from Greenwich and 56.35 south longitude. This gale No. 5 was between 53 and 54 of south longitude.

Saturday, 23rd February

Sea smooth, rain small, but very cold. Going along well tacking, the wind being nearly North. At midday we were nearly opposite the entrance of the Straits of *Magalhães*.[25] At 4 P.M. we all went on deck to put the ship about seawards and get more canvass on her, which we had scarce done and let the reefs out; when down came a heavy sou'wester and it was all we could do to get in our canvass, especially the new mainsail being the first time it was furled. We soon saw a gale had set in and the sea got up frightfully and we were obliged to lay to under a close reefed main topsail, fore topmast, staysail and main trisel. Pig dead, eaten by rats. Had been ill.

---

[24] Giving a hundred excuses and apologies.

[25] I.e., Magellan. Magalhães, as was his Portuguese name, was from the North of Portugal, more precisely Sabrosa which is in the heart of the Demarcated Douro Region where Port Wine is made.

Sunday, 24th February – 5th storm

Storm still heavy, saw the American ship to leeward standing head to land. Seas sweeping over us, one came over the bows right aft bringing the dog with it, he biting and snapping at the water, with but few opportunities of giving her head way, very heavy seas. A sea went to the top of the main trisel and several washed the quarterdeck.

Monday, 25th February

Storm still raging, continued all day, at times furiously. This is the 5th gale we have had and also the strongest, besides which we are on a lee shore, fortunately, at a good distance. From midday yesterday to midday today, we drifted 44 miles towards it, but even yet about 130 miles west from it. (From Cape Pillar, the entrance to the Straits of Magellan, but about 30 miles south of it). Towards evening it moderated and more sail was set but at night had to reef again.

Tuesday, 26th February

During night going almost a northerly course, squally but sun out. Sea not quite so high. Frequent showers but of short duration. At 10 A.M. met a barque going south shewed flag scarcely distinguishable, but made out to be English. By midday we had made a very good days' work being very near our course about 150 miles of Northing.

Wednesday, 27th February – 6th storm

Going almost North but towards midday blowing pretty hard. At 11 the strap that fastens the foretopsail yard to the mast broke, and the yard got adrift, but soon got set to rights. At midday we have made about the same course and distance as yesterday, but being only 60 miles from land (Isla Madre de Dios[26]) on the lee, we tacked under close reefed sails. At dusk laid to with a heavy north.

---

[26] They had gone round Cape Horn and sailed some ways up the very southwest coast of Chile.

Thursday, 28ᵗʰ February

6ᵗʰ storm – 2 days. Laid to under a close reefed main and fore stay sails, terrific sea and wind, more than any we have yet had. The sea frequently washing over our quarterdeck. At midday had a sight, have drifted about 30 miles back on exactly the same track we passed yesterday but are a little further from land. At 4 o'clock full dead calm with very heavy sea, ship rolling enough to bring down all her hamper, she often dipped with her bulwarks under and twice with the rail of the quarter deck under, lifting up the boats on the davits. Large whale seen. At dusk a gentle breeze. We going NorthWest. Found my slippers.

Friday, 1ˢᵗ March

Sun out, occasionally warmer, a clear morning smooth sea, all sail set, a few showers of rain but going North west and by north. At midday were about 2 miles north of where we were on the 27ᵗʰ, but more to the westward. Clark complaining that no one on board likes him, few of the men respect him or even with him good morning. Left off one of my blankets and one pair stockings.

Saturday, 2ⁿᵈ March

Morning small rain, but wind fair, at noon cleared up and sun out, have made 153 miles of our course and are opposite the *Golfo de Penas*. Towards evening wind better, going 8½ knots at times with a reef in our topsails and no stunsails – 150 miles west, Southwest of *Cabo Tres Montes*.

Sunday, 3ʳᵈ March

Fair wind, beautiful clear day, going along beautifully. At midday have made … miles of our course. Sea as smooth as possible. Very warm, took off heavy blanket and flannel drawers.[27]

---

[27] English, not American, word for underpants.

Monday, 4th March

Beautiful day, sea smooth as glass, but very little wind. In the afternoon, John shot a large porpoise. Bannister and I went in a gig about 3 miles after it but without success. Got on board at sunset. Curious birds.

Tuesday, 5th March

Almost calm but we slipped along 3 to 4 knots. A Brig in sight following in our wake, making oars. At night, row forward. Peixoto had struck a boy and the Contramestre went and reproved him for doing so, having already often prohibited these men from beating boys; men abusive and particularly Peixoto and Miguel so the Contramestre went forward again and words ensuing we all ran forward. Miguel had just come up from the forecastle where he had been to fetch his knife which Bannister took from him; both threatened what they would do to the Boatswain but desisted when we went forward. Shark astern.

Wednesday, 6th March

Brig close astern and at 8 A.M. spoke to her. She is a Yankee going to California, dirty fore royal, his chronometer out by a jar, he shewed 79 we are in 77, we set him right. At noon, today, we are opposite Valdivia in the Latitude of Figueira.[28] Brig went in towards the land, she is from Boston in 110 days. Carried away stunsail boom. Cloudy evening, wind Northeast for the first time.

Thursday, 7th March

Fine clear day, going along finely at 7 to 9 knots and at times 9½. Fresh wind from Southeast, almost astern, in the evening it came on

---

[28] Reference to Figueira da Foz in Portugal, south of Porto and close to Coimbra, which is at the same latitude in the Northern Hemisphere as Valdivia is in the Southern Hemisphere. Eliza's father George, who married Fanny FLOWER, had a brandy distillery in Figueira where they lived until they moved to Porto in 1857. Figueira, with its fine beach and proximity to the waterfowl-rich Aveiro waterways, was also very popular during the summer and the shooting season.

very fresh, carried away another stunsail boom and at dusk reduced us to our lower canvasses, viz. 2 topsails, main and foresails and jib, with one reef in our topsails with which she goes 7 to 8 knots and sometimes a little more. The sky perfectly clear. The sea changes colour – more clay coloured.

We are about 70 miles from land and several on board said they saw it but I could not. A large ship crossed our bows at some distance going right head to land apparently bound to *Conceição*[29]. I made an oar and hand spike but in the midst of my work was unwell and had to break off. Today at midday opposite *Isla Santa Maria*.

---

[29] I.e., Concepción, a coastal town south of Valparaíso.

VALPARAISO, CHILE

Friday, 8th March

Sighted the land and at midday opposite the River Maule.

Saturday, 9th March

Opposite the river Tanguen at midday.

Sunday, 10th March

Off the bar and at night close in by lighthouse.

Monday, 11th March

Entered and anchored near the British Hulk in Valparaiso at 6 A.M. with 64 days voyage and after breakfast received the visits and disembarked.

*   *   *

We first on land and saw the sign of Macfarlane and Searle over the door of a store near the mole and after enquiring, found it the Searle to be John's cousin, John C. Searle, who received his relation and us very well giving us all a standing invitation to their house. This firm have a larger establishment for victualling ships, the first in the place and have the contract with the navy.

We next presented our letter of introduction to Mr. Thos. Garland[30] in the house of Myers Bland & Co., Calle de la Aduana No.

---

[30] Probably a relative of the Garland family who formed a partnership in Lisbon, in 1775, with a General Laidley. The Porto office was opened in 1897. The firm at this time acted as steamship agents for the Booth and Cunard lines. Most cargo was loaded into Douro lighters and then towed to Leixões Harbour to be loaded on board. For this purpose, Garland and Laidley were partners in a Lighter and Towage Company. This company owned some 10 sea-going lighters, 3 tugs and 2 passenger launches. One of the managers was Francis Errington Dawson, a name that crops up under Rawes & Co., another famous shipping firm. There was a strong family connection between the two firms as F.E. Dawson's sister married Stanley Rawes whose sister in turn married his brother, Alfred Dawson. The firm Garland & Laidley still exists in Porto and Lisbon today.

91, where we were all well received and introduced to Mr. Dogues[31] the principal partner in Valparaiso. Were invited John, Joel, Laidley and I to dine at Garlands at 6, took stroll till that time but got into the lower part of the town, lowest at least in character though situated on the sides of the steep hills, English generally understood. Evening at Garlands, came on board at 9 P.M.

Tuesday, 12th March

Took samples of our cargo to Myers Bland & Co. to buy and dispose part of it; all dine at Macfarlane's at 4. Our flag bothers every one, some call us Hamburguese on account of the castle in it, but most rate us Brazilians.[32]

Wednesday, 13th March

Men grumbling, want 1 month's wages; roaming about town, but this time saw the *alamendral*[33] or west end, nice place and people. Governed by D. M. Blanco Admiral and General, and good force of *serenos* and *vigilantes*.[34] Met with John Tarnels and Francisco Semperio of San Francisco.

Thursday, 14th March

Whilst John and I were at Myers, Bland & Co., were told a steamer was just ready to start for Panama which expected to catch last Packet, so John wrote home and I wrote a note to Liz and a few lines in it to my Father, but hurriedly, we had not time to come on board for the letters we had written.

---

[31] Could this name be Dagge? There was a Richard Dagge as a merchant in Porto at the time and the family was an extensive one.

[32] The Portuguese coat-of-arms that is on the flag includes a castle. The other reference is to the great German trading port of Hamburg.

[33] Old Portuguese word for a wide, elegant avenue, usually planted with poplars. *Alameda* is the Spanish equivalent.

[34] Forms of policemen and watchmen.

Today our men all knocked off working as we would not give them a month's wages and tried to get away so we were obliged to keep watch over them to prevent their running away. I went to complain to the Captain of the Port (Aurelio); he was busy boarding the numerous vessels that kept coming in.

Friday, 15ᵗʰ March

Men still off work, we stopped their grub, the *Moços*[35] only at work. Captain of Port too busy to attend to us.

Saturday, 16ᵗʰ March

Drills and print sold and preparations made for discharging part of our cargo as part of the wines are also sold. Eliza's Birthday. Invited to dine tomorrow at Macfarlane's and ride after dinner, but refused.

Sunday, 17ᵗʰ March

Boys and us busy heaving at anchor as the ship had dragged, so that when I got on shore it was too late for Church. Today there were races near the lighthouse and all the fine folks, Gentlemen andLadies were going there. I dined with John and Clark at Macfarlane's and rode with them on Macfarlane's horses to the end of the alamendral. John slept on shore.

Monday, 18ᵗʰ March

Captain of Port on board at 9 A.M. and hearing the story from the men of John's stopping their grub, appeared to side with them. After he left we went to his office with Garland and the Portuguese laws[36]. After a little palaver, he gave an order to his *ajudante*[37], to take those on board to prison, as many as we wanted, so off we came with

---

[35] Boys
[36] Probably consular officials or similar.
[37] Aide.

him and gave into his charge, António, Pires, Miguel and Peixoto, who were forthwith walked off to prison. Dined at Garland's.

Tuesday, 19th March

All hands at work, not wishing to follow the other three; had also 6 men from shore to help at 1 dollar each per day. The south wind gave us a specimen of its powers by blowing furiously as it often does here during the summer, which is very near over here, it begins about 10 A.M. and blows till 4 or 5 P.M. with such fury as often to set the ships adrift, and the town is enveloped in one cloud of dust, windows and doors are all closed till it is over. It is believed to be very unhealthy causing much ossification of the heart for which few are clear. The place is considered in general unhealthy for ladies more so than men, but the interior appears to be more healthy.

Wednesday, 20th March

Discharged part of cargo sold by Myers, Bland & Co., it is taken on shore by launches for the use of which we pay 4 dollars and 1 dollar each to the men to work it.

Sunday, 24th March

Great preparations on shore for the devotions of the ensuing week. I went to Church with Clark and heard the discourse by Mr. Armstrong, pretty good, met Mrs. Garland there. Coming out of church, we saw the Packet from Panama coming in but did not get our letters till night when I received one from Liz in one from my Father dated 1st December 1849. All well. Dined at Macfarlane's.

Valparaiso, Tuesday 9th April

On shore early finishing getting off things to the ship so as to try to get her to sea today. Myers, Bland & Co. kept us till after 4 P.M. ere we got our accounts settled with them. I then wrote a note to Liz and Father and enclosed it in a letter of Clark's to Rawes [*sic*]. At 6 P.M.

Clark and I came off to ship, where we found John and Laidley with J.C. Searle and all our passengers.

We got the anchor up and out, we went under double reefed topsails with a strong south wind, the ship rolled very much, having a heavy deck load. We had on board twenty-two *Proa*[38] passengers and aft Captain Gardiner and his wife.

At sea, Wednesday 10ᵗʰ April

Strong breeze aft, going along beautifully, but rolling much. I took charge of the *dispensa*[39] with António and José Maria.

Thursday, 11ᵗʰ April

Our Chilean passengers began to show themselves, but still very sick.

Friday, 12ᵗʰ April

Less wind, rather on the quarter, going easier but with a starboard list. Whale fired at.

Saturday, 13ᵗʰ April

Becalmed; water as smooth as oil, beautiful sundown giving the sea the appearance of a lake of gold and silver.

Sunday, 14ᵗʰ April

Towards night a gentle breeze, sermon read.

Monday, 15ᵗʰ April

I felt unwell, headache. A very large turtle seen by the mate.

Tuesday, 16ᵗʰ April

Gentle south breeze, busy making new gaff-topsail. I still unwell.

---

[38] Steerage

[39] Stewarage

Wednesday, 17th April

Very warm, I better having applied cold water to head, obliged to put on lighter clothes.

Thursday, 18th April

No news. I washing clothes. After this the voyage continued without incident worthy of notice, till we cross the line[40] which we did on the 4th May in the evening, in 107 degrees, the wind being always aft.

Saturday, 4th May

Slept under a boat. My birthday. António complaining of men throwing the meat in his face, row about food. Contramestre took part with men and mate flew in a passion against him and men. Our carpenter has been two days making an oar, so John called him to account for it and came aft asking Captain Gardiner how many oars a man should make in a day, to which he answered his carpenter made four. John said ours takes two days to make one. When our carpenter who had come after him, came up in an insolent manner and said "Come fair play, two watches and not two days", Searle said "Don't speak to me in that way or I'll give you a box on the ear." "You daring", says Chips[41], so Searle gave him one. "I dare you to do that again" says Chips, so John gave him some more to settle his impudence; one of them cut his ear so Chips dipped his finger in the blood and held it up to John's view and would have continued to be insolent had not Bannister pushed him forward. These were the entertainments on my 27th birthday!

Albacores, and I speared a bonito seen on the 6th.

---

[40] The equator, I presume.

[41] Nickname for carpenters.

Wednesday, May 8th

From 4th till today, wind little but fair today, almost calm; caught a shark about 7 feet long and John shot at it aft, it was hooked and killed it. We have often seen whales and shot at them; this evening we saw a swordfish and caught two bonitos.

At night about 12 P.M. a storm came suddenly on, wind and rain. The ship was put before it and soon blew over. I was caught in the wet for the rain pelted through the boat seams and ere I would cover myself with a quilt and bounce out, I was wet through, perspiring at the time. The rain fell in torrents and water was caught in every utensil, but the heat below was intolerable. I laid on the bench but could not sleep. Making at times 8 knots per hour.

Thursday, 9th May

All hands washing clothes, showery all day, catching water from the frequent showers. Lots of fish about, but one caught, clouds of flying fish. Caught a shark 7-foot long and bonito.

Friday, 10th May

All hands washing clothes, laughable figures. Fish about, one caught.

Saturday, 11th May

Gentle but steady breezes aft, cloudy and very close.

Sunday, 12th May

Frequent showers, very close, winds from North to North West, but very light. Row with mate, Bannister, boatswain, António and men quarrelling.

Monday, 13th May

Calm, light winds, composed letter to Liz and commenced little boat. Ship to the East seen.

Tuesday, 14th May

Rain showers day and night, wind light and variable. Bannister harpooned a queer fish 7-foot this shape *sketch* (*jamanta*[42]), but he got off. Caught a bonito with small flying fish in it. Wind chopped around all night.

Wednesday, 15th May

In morning, light NorthWest winds but at dinner time, wind changes to North East so we suppose we are in the North East trades[43].

Thursday, 16th May

Trades much Northing in them, row with Clark and Gardener, calling each other drunkards and working at boat ribs, verily commenced boat.

Friday, 17th May

Ship in sight on the weather box, by noon we were opposite her distance 7 miles, flagged her, American barque on same course as us but going slower.

Saturday 18th May

Working at boat, trades much Northing, they are driving us up to the westward, ship continues to make 4½ inches of water per hour, suppose through a rat hole, no ship in sight. Net finished.

Sunday, 19th May

Almost calm, *o vento escace*[44].

Monday, 20th May

Row on board. António threw up charge of Dispensa, refusing to act as *dispensero*[45] on account of barrel of wine going fast and rows

---

[42] Devilfish, large manta ray.

[43] *Sic.* trade winds

[44] There is little wind.

[45] Dispenser of provisions, i.e., steward.

with the people. I called him and talked to him for having sent him for wood, he refused to give it out, so I told him to go forward and consider by tomorrow whether or not we should change places and he be master and I servant. Searle went forward and threatened to put him in irons if he did not turn to. The men laughed at him, I and one and all were ripe for a row and defending António if such had been attempted. I prepared for it and was low and (...*illegible*...) from me when António came to know what to get for dinner tomorrow. Mutinous omens forward suspended, pilot fish alongside. Laidley and Clark made friends after *cachasse*[46]. Have 5 timbers, stem, stern and keep for boat made.

Tuesday, 21ˢᵗ May

In morning António came to tell me that according to orders he had considered and resolved again to continue as dispensero on consideration that he alone should have the run of the *paiol*[47] as then he could be responsible. Agreed. Got keel box and stern put together. Off boat and placed for working on quarterdeck. Stiff breeze NorthEast.

Wednesday, 22ⁿᵈ May

Seven months today since we left Porto, named boat Fairy and got half of her timbers up. Working hard. Vessel in sight on our western quarter.

Thursday, 23ʳᵈ May

Up early and worked hard, by eight had 13 timbers out of the 16 in the boat and inside stringers up. Vessel in sight to leeward. Stiff breeze, North-North East, taught bowline.

Saturday, 1ˢᵗ June

Boat (Fairy) finished by night of carpentering, ready to caulk.

---

[46] Sic. cachaça: raw sugar cane spirit or brandy.

[47] Stores

Sunday, 2nd June

Sail in sight to windward, wind N. E., we taught bowline, we shewed colours, schooner bore down to speak to us, under English colours and about 2 P.M. laid to a little ahead when we came up to her, spoke to her and gave her the longitude 143, she had 141. She is the *Sir John Franklin* of Hobart Town, lastly from Wahoo, one of the Sandwich Islands in 14 days from the last Port, she is a schooner, 23 tons: carrying lumber and bricks and looks little bigger than our long boat.

Monday, 3rd June

Schooner *Sir John Franklin* astern, we laid to being little wind for her to come up, then went on board of her to hear the news. She gives news from California a month old and 14 days. Gold abundant as ever. Lumber cheap, drinkables dear, everyone gone to the mines. We were about two hours on board. Captain has his wife and 2 children on board and 4 men. Gave us Honolulu papers of 1st May 1850.

Tuesday, 4th June

Schooner astern and to leeward, we becalmed all day or nearly so. Freshened towards evening. Reminded Mrs. Garland to use rainwater.

Wednesday, 5th June

Schooner not seen, steady 4 knot breeze west early, all sails set. Began to line the launch. Gardiner took upon himself to set Jack[48] about his own work and Searle and he had to jaw about it. Gardiner got restive and tried to kick but I sent the boy to his work and told Gardiner that if he did not mind what he was about we would have to put him in irons. Gardiner answered "I dare you to it, I'll put a bullet through you first." Bannister spent the rest of the day with Gardiner, they two are hand and glove now. Ligeira pupped 5 pups.

---

[48] A young boy who shipped with them. HEW never mentions his last name or gives any further details.

Thursday, 6th June

Bannister and Gardiner hand and glove and from conversation heard, we find it so, remarked also by Harris. All three, Mr. and Mrs. Gardiner and Bannister, all refuse salt food.

Friday, 7th June

Bannister and Gardiner hand and glove. At dinner Mrs. Gardiner complained to Searle that she could not eat salt food as we had both pigs and fowls on board and wished to know the reason of a change which she said had taken place lately, as till then we had done all in our power to make her comfortable. Searle answered her fair and promised to look to that. A pig was being killed at the time.

Monday, 10th June

Becalmed with smooth sea.

Tuesday, 11th June

Breeze freshened from North to a gale towards evening. We had to close reef two topsails and with a staysail and main trisel, carried on all night.

Wednesday, 12th June

Storm continued, but with clear sky, high sea and in morning she shipped a sea which came into my berth. Towards evening it abated and came from N.W.

ARRIVING IN SAN FRANCISCO

Thursday, 13th June

By 4 in the morning, we saw land on the lee bow being the Farallon Islands, ran through them and made the mainland to the north of the Port, several other vessels, say 8, bearing for the port. We also bore down to the port of San Francisco and were the first in and anchored at 1 P.M., near the lighthouse in the port of San Francisco. Searle and I landed and were on shore till 6 P.M. N.B. Pilotage $108.00 on $8.00 per foot water the ship draws. Health visit came. $20.00 to pay him and demands $2.00 a head for steerage passengers and $3.00 for cabin, us included, also $2.00 a head for the sailors.

Friday, 14th June

At 9 A.M. Searle and Clark, Laidley and Bannister went ashore. Soon after a fire broke out in the town, about $3,000,000.00 worth of property burnt down[49].

---

[49] The third great fire in the city, the alarm actually sounded at 8 a.m.. The cause was a defective flue in a bakery in the rear of the Merchant's Hotel on Kearny street, between Sacramento and Clay, was the starting point. Unfortunately one of the fiercest winds of the season was blowing and in a few hours all between Clay and California from Kearny to the water's edge was made of flames. The entire loss was estimated to be $3,500,000.

Monday, 17th June

Closed and posted my letter No. 68 to Liz, one to Uncle John,[50] and one to my Father, sent from packet, written on the 15th.

Monday, 15th July

Closed and posted my letter No. 69 to Liz and one to my Father dated 13th instant, enclosed to Prescott Bros. and Co. Manchester.[51]

Saturday, 20th July

Received our first amount of gold dust, one ounce for $16.00 in pay for Brandy.

Saturday, 27th July

Received the following letters from Packet from Mrs. W. Wilby[52] dated Vizella, 30th December 1849. John Wilby[53], Lisbon, 7th March 1850. Liz, No. 85 and its P.S. 25th December to 12th January 1850, viz. Valparaiso, and No. 80 of 7th February 1850, in an envelope on which is written 19th February, all well, with news of Mrs. Bannister's death.

Tuesday, 30th July

Closed and posted my No. 70 to Liz commenced 27th instant acknowledging receipt of the above two letters. Also wrote to W.B. Liot, London and wrote to Mrs. And Mrs. W. Wilby 30th July in answer to the above.

Monday, 5th August

Row about dogs and to loaded rifle to shoot (…*illegible*…) it went off a few inches above my head and entered the cornice of the Cabin.

---

[50] Possibly a reference to John Van Dam Searle, a merchant of Porto, but most likely to John Wilby.

[51] Cloth merchants, represented in Porto by James Rawes.

[52] Sarah Jane Biglands Wilby, William Wilby's 2nd wife and HEW's stepmother.

[53] John Wilby m. to Mary Chaster, HEW's uncle and living in Lisbon as agent for the Bible Society.

Tuesday, 6th August

Received a threatening letter from Searle and Clark about dogs, Saturday night. P.S. added to it expressing their intention to shoot them if not remedied by tomorrow noon. I happened to mention that I had done their drudgery of the ship (being in my bed). Searle flew into a rage and threatened if he had me out in the cab in he would kick me and suchlike, cursing and swearing at me like mad.

Thursday, 8th August

Last night wrote Searle and Gardiner a letter in answer to theirs which I delivered this morning after landing Lias and Ligeira. Read it aloud commenting on it, cursing and alleging to (as he said) to the mischief I made, and on reading my complaints of their cursing and swearing, calling me a blasted hypocrite. After breakfast, I landed with Clark, took pup to Gibb[54]'s and had a chat there.

*   *   *

Went to post and got my letters, viz. one from W.W. Porto, 2nd May 1850 with news of Mrs. Bigland's death.[55] A little letter from Louisa G. Wilby[56], Eliza's No. 87 closed 12th April, acknowledging receipt of my No. 65 from Rio per the "Sacramento", dated 22nd Dec. 1849, also a postscript to Liz's No. 87 dated 23rd April 1850, also Liz's No. 88 closed 14th May 1850 acknowledging receipt of my No. 66 written from Rio on 4th January 1850 at sailing.[57]

---

[54] There were several Gibb or Gibbs in SF at the time who could fit this person (see full list attached), but I am inclined to: Gibb, Daniel, merchant, Central wharf.
[55] I presume this was William Wilby's mother-in-law.
[56] Louisa Georgiana, HEW's step-sister.
[57] This Diary begins on 14th January 1850, already at sea. I presume they sailed from Lisbon to Rio de Janeiro and then made their way south prior to their rounding Cape Horn. Rio would have been a usual trading stop.

Thursday, 15th August

Gave Searle my letter to Liz No. 71 and saw him enclose it in his to Searle and Sons[58]. I had a letter partly written to Whiteley[59], but did not finish it in time to send.

Friday, 16th August

The *Macaista*[60] or Portuguese barque, *Nossa Senhora das Dores*, came in and anchored astern of us, from Macao with assorted cargo. 3 months' voyage, met with three typhoons, Chinese for storms.

Saturday, 17th August

Captain of the above vessel came to deposit his papers with Consul Searle[61], and says a Portuguese Brig is also expected from the same place and he reports pirates off the coast of China, who it is supposed have made free with several sloops or biggers, which have left Macao for this place and not arrived here. I took the turns out of the chains to move up by order of the Captain of the Port.

Sunday, 18th August

Went over to the island[62] with Wynn[63] and Bannister in the launch and Fairy.

---

[58] This is the first mention of such a company, presumably of Porto. Requires searching of Porto Commercial Registry Records.

[59] Rev. Edward Whiteley (1794-1875), British chaplain in Porto and head of the British School.

[60] Portuguese, meaning from Macao, the Portuguese colony in the Far East, next to China.

[61] John Searle was appointed Portuguese Consul in San Francisco on 17 May 1849 and Henry Edward Wilby, Vice-Consul, 20 Jan 1850. Source: *Annuário Portuguez – Histórico Biográphico e Diplomático. Uma Synapse de Tratados e Convenções*, p. 94. Ed. Typographia da Revista Universal, Rua dos Fanqueiros 82, Lisbon, 1855. Courtesy of Joan Wilby.

[62] Angel Island in San Francisco Bay?

[63] J.B. Wynn, listed as a partner in Searle & Wynn, Commission Merchants, 127 California Street. Source: 1852-53 San Francisco Directory

Having agreed with the Captain of the *Burmah* for him to get men and move us up to another berth and he to run the risk all for $110.00, he came with his men and got up one anchor, but as it came on to blow, left the other down till tomorrow.

Tuesday, 20th August

The Captain came and moved us up to near Rincorn Point[64] where I suppose the old ship will rest her bones for some time to come. We hoisted a red flag with a white ball in the middle, which will henceforward be our signal.

❦

---

[64] «THE CITY'S CROWDED HARBOR. Our harbor is now literally crowded with ships, and but a very indefinite idea of their number can be obtained from the city. To course through them, from Clark's to Rincon Point, to take a position out in the harbor a view them altogether is the only way. The coup d'oeil is most superb, and the bosom of a San Franciscan cannot fail to swell with pride at the evidence of the commercial importance of his city.» In: *Daily Alta California*, Tuesday Morning, August 13, 1850

THE DOCKS, DEVASTATING
FIRES AND HANGINGS

Saturday, 24th August

Went to *Sonsoleto* [*sic*. Sausalito], saw hares and Pelicans.

Saturday 31st August

Portuguese Brig *Amizade*[65] entered from Macao with a crew of Chinamen, deposited her papers with Searle as Consul.

Gave up to Captain Passos the papers of the No*va Pagueti* and made out his *Matricula*[66], she being ready to sail the day after tomorrow for Manila and charged him $45.00 for their consular fees. Took an office at Gibb's brick buildings at $150.00 per month from 1st September.

*   *   *

Closed the following letters from the mail tomorrow to G.B.' Carr in the name of the house, offering our services and enclosing a letter for Mr. John Wilby to E. Wilby[67] in the name of the house, advising a remittance to him of about 260 pounds and also the same, a private letter. In this I post a letter I had written on the 15th instant for the Reverend E. Whiteley, another for my Father, Lavinia[68] and Louisa (of this date) and another to Eliza, No. 72, in this I put a gold dollar. Making in all, four letters in Carr's.

---

[65] Interesting, as this is most like the ship of the same name that became infamous folllowing the takeover of the ship by its "cargo" of slaves.

[66] Registration.

[67] I presume this is Edward Wilby, HEW's grandfather/great uncle, considering the reference in George Frederick Naylor's Notebook to the fact that his uncle had apparently lost a lot of money to the Americans. Seeing as how the same Edward Wilby was both William Wilby's father-in-law (1st marriage to Ann Wilby, his cousin, mother to HEW) and uncle, it would not be extreme to suppose he might have been encouraged to invest in his grandson's trading ventures in California. Source of Notebook: Roberta O'Brien.

[68] Lavinia Anne Wilby, HEW's sister.

Sunday, 1st September

At 4:30 A.M. this morning, Clark was taken very ill, by 9 we got him on shore to Gibb's and called a Doctor, who bled him and ordered leeches to his chest which was in a high state of inflammation. The bleeding gave immediate relief, we bought a dozen leeches for $22.00, they would not bite – Aubrey[69] went and got us a dozen others, just arrived (a present) which took beautifully and did Clark good.

Tuesday, 3rd September

Clark better, up, but weak.

Thursday, 5th September

Packet in but no letters for any of us. Crew of the *Amizade* bolted. Searle got them all taken up and taken on board by the treaty with Portugal, taking it out of the hands of the authorities here to do anything but assist the Consul when required by him to do so.

Monday, 9th September

Very wintry looking day. Strong S.W. wind. Cold and dreary. Intimated by Harbourmaster to move again, further out.

Tuesday, 10th September

Fine again. Avila (our Mate) in, complaining with three other Portuguese about the American Brig, *Arabian*. We made the purchase for them and Searle gives them the Portuguese flag.

Sunday, 15th September

Posted my letter to Liz No. 73 of from 13th to 14th instant enclosed in one to Aunt Elizabeth Rawes[70], sent in J. Barnes and Co. letter via Prescott Bros.

---

[69] "Aubrey" Gibb/ Aubrey Laidley?

[70] Mary Elizabeth Wilby, daughter of Edward Wilby above and sister to HEW's mother, married James Rawes of Porto.

Tuesday, 17ᵗʰ September⁷¹

Woke up at 4:30 A.M. fire on shore, went to it, houses burning like tinder. Fire stopped by 9 A.M. About 200 houses burnt. Luckily no wind. At midday, heard of an opportunity of writing by a steamer to Panama which would catch the Packet, so wrote a few lines to Mrs. Rawes and in them enclosed a few to Eliza informing them of the fire and our not being sufferers of it.

Friday and Saturday, 20ᵗʰ and 21ˢᵗ of September

Very wet, dull weather, but not cold.

Sunday, 22ⁿᵈ September

Beautiful day, sun out, awnings spread and very pleasant. I went to church which had been enlarged and was well attended.

---

⁷¹ This was the fourth great fire in nine months. It started in the Philadelphia House on Jackson street near the Washington market, and swept away most of the blocks between Pacific and Washington, Dupont and Montgomery streets. Nearly all the houses were one-story wooden structures and burnt fiercely. On Washington street, between Dupont and Kearny, the brick walls of the Alta California building, erected after the May fire, stopped the flames and led to better materials being used in rebuilding.

Monday, 23rd September

Received Liz's No. 89 and its P.S. from 16th May to 20th June, acknowledging receipt of my letter of 14th March, announcing my arrival in Valparaiso. Liz received my long letter No. 67 of 29th January 1850 on the 17th June 1850, from Valparaiso. Same day it was resolved that John Searle should go to Porto by next Packet.

Saturday, 28th September

Appointed *Vice-Consul de Portugal* and presented to Col. Collier, Comptroller of Customs and recognised by him in my official capacity.[72]

Tuesday, 1st October

John Searle left for Panama[73] per *California*[74]. I gave John letters of introduction to R. Ackerley, D. Campbell, W.P. Liet, G.B. Carr, the D'Almaine and Co., and Perry at Panama to the latter, I sent the note of introduction that Liet wrote me to him.

*   *   *

---

[72] Interesting, as official records show he was appointed Vice-Consul on 20 Jan 1850. Perhaps he was not so informed by John Searle at the time?

[73] San Francisco to Panama via steamer took approximately 15 days. Crossing of the Isthmus was by canoe, mule and foot, usually in very bad conditions on even worse roads. From the East Coast of Panama to the East Coast of the US, usually New York, was another 15 days. Shipping magnates such as George Law, Aspinwall/Pacific Mail Line and Cornelius Vanderbilt formally established steam ship passenger routes to cover that route. Pacific Mail Lines focused on the crossing at Panama, while Vanderbilt's Independent Line crossed Nicaragua, albeit shorter, an even more unpleasant and dangerous route. No wonder so many preferred to risk going around the Horn!

[74] SS *California* Builder: William H. Webb, New York, 1848. Original Owner: Pacific Mail Steamship Company. Launch: May 19, 1848. 199 feet, 1,057 tons, 2 decks, 3 masts, round stern, 1057 tons, with a capacity of 210 passengers. She had a gleaming black hull (copper-sheathed below the waterline), white upper works, red paddle wheels, and plenty of polished brass, she was a delight to behold. Sources: Maritime Heritage and APL (American Pacific Lines) Webpage.

I sent by him, to Liz, my letter No. 74, concluded 28th September and closed 1st October, also a specimen of California gold I got off the fat Chilena[75], 1 round dark coloured pearl, 7 small black pearls, 1 lead-coloured *cabaça*[76]-shaped pearl and one with outer rim, round bottom pearl. By him also wrote to my Father and in his letter enclosed one to A.F. Sealey and one to John Atkinson[77], both of 28th September and I delivered to his charge a little tin box directed to my Father with the following specimens of California gold and directed each as under, and 8 pearls, these to distribute to Ma[78] and sisters. By him also wrote to Uncle John and sent him a California Gold, one to Aunt, John and one to Cousin Jane Chaster.[79] and a coloured pearl for the latter.

Thursday, 10th October

At night taken with gripes, vomiting, purging, shivering, cramps, took jingers [*sic. jinja*[80]] and was well next day. Bought 150 bags sugar.

Saturday, 12th October

Received letter from Father and Lav. Of 5th July acknowledging receipt of my letters from Valparaiso. This letter came by Gregory's, experts from New York, where it was forwarded by Osborn Bros. And

---

[75] Spanish, meaning Chilean woman – could be a person or a ship!

[76] Gourd-shaped

[77] John Atkinson, merchant of Porto and friend of Rev. Edward Whiteley's, came to Porto with him from YKS. The Rev. married (2) John Atkinson's daughter Eliza (1825-1877) and John Atkinson's son Edward married the Rev.'s daughter Emily by his first wife, deceased. Thus they were both father-in-laws and brothers-in-laws.

[78] Sarah Anne Biglands Wilby, HEW's step-mother.

[79] She could be either daughter of HEW's aunt Mary Wilby Chaster and thus sister to his cousin Henry who married (2) Hannah Stott in 1852. Alternatively she could be a daughter of HEW's aunt Jane Emma WILBY, daughter of Edward and Anne Wilby) who married George Chaster, presumably brother of Thomas Chaster (married Mary Elizabeth Wilby, HEW's aunt) and Mary Chaster (married John Wilby, HEW's uncle).

[80] A kind of strong brandy made from morello cherries.

the express man had been some days in finding me. I saw in newspaper, notice of the barque *Guilford*, Captain Thorpe from Lisbon being in Rio Janeiro on 9th July on her way hither.

A city directory first published in this town of San Francisco.

I this day signed a sailing letter granting the Portuguese Flag to the American barque and brig brought by the pumpkin-faced man for José Vicente Jorge of Macao and also signed Matricula of the Portuguese Brig *Filial*.

Tuesday, 15th October

Posted my letter No. 75 to Liz.

Friday, 25th October

Received Liz's letter No. 90 with bad news from her on the 20th of July 1850. She received the few lines I wrote from Valparaiso just as we were ready to sail.

Monday, 28th October

Move ship, head inshore.

Tuesday, 29th October

Celebration of the entry of California as one of the U.S. Grand procession in which I walked with the other Consuls. *Sagamore* blown up, *Mariposa* is also a wreck up the river having been run down by the steamer *West Point*.

Wednesday, 30th October

Hospital burnt down.

Friday, 1st November

Closed and posted my letter to Liz No. 76 and posted my letter to my Father, ½ a sheet dated 30th October.

Saturday, 2nd November

Towards evening it came on to blow a gale of wind from the (…
illegible…) and very cold, considerable swell in the bay, an awful fire on
the *contracosta*[81], lots of ducks and geese crossing over there and have
been for this last fortnight. They are selling here at $1.00 each.

Friday, 8th November

Received Liz's letter No. 91 dated 29th August to 3rd September
1850, acknowledging receipt of my No. 68, closed 17th June 1850, with
news of our arrival in California, this she received on the 26th August
1850, mentions my Father having received by letter from here also
and having informed her of my arrival. Louisa reached home. Mama
expected early in September.

Along with Liz's letter came a letter from Jim Garland, dated 7th
September, acknowledging receipt of our first letter from here as the
Packet came in yesterday, this letter was exactly two months from the
writer's hand to our here! Quick eh? In San Francisco, the weather is
cold, shipping preparing for winter.

Sunday, 10th NovembSer

At 8 A.M. this morning, Gibb came on board to tell me that his
ship the *Burmah* was sinking and to request that I would immediately
let go my moorings, (that is of the *Sophia*, Captain Wilby[82]) and drop
alongside of her to save what cargo we can of hers. I got up directly,
unshackled my chains made them fast and dropped alongside her as
they hauled her up; she was sinking fast.

We set to work and got as much out of her as we could, about 100
Tons, which lightened her and left the leaks above water so that before

---

[81] Portuguese for the coast on the other side of the bay.
[82] A search of the Maritime Heritage Project website reveals no ship or Captain
by these names entering San Francisco during the timeframe in question, but
then, neither does it mention the *Bella Pernambucana* or any of the ships flying a
Portuguese flag mentioned in this diary.

next morning the pumps sucked (the men who worked them got $1.50 each per hour). I had 3 men ½ the day to work at $5.00 each. José Pamplona Corte Real from Fayal[83] came on board to stay the winter for his grub only, to do usual work on board, but when men are called *extraordinaire*[84] he is to receive the same as they do.

Monday, 11ᵗʰ November

We worked till late last night and were at it early this morning again with 6 men and took out about 500 Tons more from the *Burmah* and stowed part, very tired, got our moorings aboard again.

Tuesday, 12ᵗʰ November

Burmah left us and returned to her moorings, leaks being above water. We busy stowing. 3 men to help.

Wednesday, 13ᵗʰ November

Stowing and taking note of cargo, 3 men to help. At work ourselves; Gibb agrees to give us $400.00 for all that is on board (storage) for one month and what remains beyond that time, to pay the regular storage $3.00 per month, 130 bags barley belonging to Beeshy came to be stored for a fortnight.

Thursday, 14ᵗʰ November

Clark today informed me that his expense of grub (of which he only then had got the account) with Gibb are $100.00 for month; this won't do! Last month my expense on board, grub for 3 always and sometimes workmen, amounted only to $71.00. We also find the rent too heavy and resolved to seek fresh quarters. Oh dear! Oh dear! Partners, the word ought to be explained in the dictionary this way; people who associate themselves in business for the mutual benefit of a firm but as a caution to all young men be it added, each generally tries

---

[83] One of the Azores islands.
[84] To work overtime or for special duties.

only to benefit himself and he who would acquit himself according to agreement is victimised; partnership ought to be avoided as much as man traps and spring guns.

Friday, 15th November

Closed my letter No. 77 to Liz commenced 8th instant, acknowledging receipt of her No. 91, giving her amongst other news, the following: a person employed 12 men at Parks Bar, 25 days and got out $75,000.00 which is here deposited at Wells and Co. bank. In Santa Cruz, not far from here, a man realised this season, $8500.00 from 6 acres of land planted with potatoes. 3 men brought on the 13th or 14th to town $80,000.00 got by them in the mines in 7 weeks.

Bullion exported from San Francisco, that is freight declared exclusive of that taken by passengers, from 1st to 13th instant:

Passenger Schooner *Caroline*	$48,000.00
Passenger Ship, Steamer *Panama* for Panama	$1,800,000.00
Passenger Ship, Steamer *Antilope*	$200,000.00

Fletcher of Porto is here, Tommy Evans also, the latter has been at the mines but no luck.

Saturday, 16th November

Boarded an English schooner *Victoria* from Liverpool, to get her consignment, but Wynn had got his through Aubrey.

Monday, 17th November

Went to the First Congregational Church[85] in the morning and heard an excellent sermon from an elderly man, native of Connecticut. Then went over the hill, past the Lake, the Presidio, to the Bar Battery, beautiful walk, got back in the afternoon, by way of the Telegraph,

---

[85] First Congregational Church, corner of Jackson and Virginia sts., Rev. T. D. Hunt, home corner of Mason and Vallejo sts.

whence there is a most beautiful view of the Bay and shipping; thence on board, Laidley and José had gone to the *Missões*[86] in the Fairy, got her aground and did not get back till very late.

Wednesday, 20th November

Yesterday morning a terrible gale of wind from the S.S.E. set in and lasted till midday today; we dragged both anchors and came side onto the bows of the *Calumet* and the *Eleanor*, smashing in our rail from stem to stern, were kept up a night laying out warps and heaving on them. Starkey Brothers' English barque about 200 yds. From us being heavy laden with iron, which shifted to one side, filled and went down, bowsprit and ½ masts are out of water being shallow.

Another vessel dragged her moorings and drifted down, across the bows of a ship, which she stove in. A schooner near us in moving in, lost her main mast and many others were in distress, being inside the line from Rincorn and Clark's points, we suffered less than the others. At midday I got with difficulty, 7 men to re-moor us but there was but time to lift and redrop our bow anchor. Wet all day and cold. Picked up a boat and sails.

Thursday, 21st November

Had three men at work all day preparing to drop fore yard and topmast and carried out a lot of old chain aft, fast to the Ledge, wet all day. All tired and knocked up.

Friday, 22nd November

Fine day. Received from packet, a letter from my Father dated 16th September 1850 from Vizella, he had received mine of 17th June on the 25th August and also mine of 13th July on 15th September. We received two letters from John Searle, who left here 1st November, one from Panama, 22nd Oct., the other from Chagres 25th. Doing well, no cholera at Panama. We also received a letter from W. S. Boughton

---

[86] Portuguese for Missions, i.e., the old Spanish missions.

acknowledging receipt of our account, sales and remittances, is pleased and by the same packet 19th September, had ordered his friends in London to secure him a place in a vessel from there to call at Porto for 200 [*sic*. quarter] Casks and 400 Octaves[87] Port. Also a letter from Tait and Clark, one from Rawes. Also a letter from (…illegible…) of London with open *apolicy*[88]. Also one from Myers, Bland & Co. of Valparaiso, acknowledging receipt of gold dust; they say Barley is very scarce but will ship some as soon as possible, though they fear we shan't gain by it.

Saturday, 23rd November

Fine morning, wet afternoon, not cold. I boarded three English vessels to no effect. The *Indiana* of Dundee from Callao with flour, the *Diana* of Glasgow from G. and Valparaiso to Gibb and a barque from Honolulu with vegetables. A few days ago Clark told me that Almeida wanted us to lend him money - $600.00 – on 24 boxes tea, it to be brought on board here, he paying freight and storage and 6% per month interest as it was worth about $1,000.00. I agreed. In the afternoon of the same day, a man came with an order from Almeida for $600.00, which Clark had left me, orders to pay. But as I had not heard of the tea going on board, I as an excuse told him to come tomorrow as the Cashier was not in.

The day after I told Clark. "It is all right" said he. I paid the man and the tea will go on board. Every day since, I asked about the tea, today see it in our offices, when in conversation, it came out that Clark had given him $1,000.00 as the holder of the tea after saying he would deliver it for $600.00, ran back and he therefore had to give the other $400.00 on it and some jewellery (most of it imitation!) this on

---

[87] Half a quarter cask. 1 shipping cask = 534 Litres; hogshead = 134 litres; octave = 67 litres

[88] Portuguese word for insurance policy.

his accord, eh! Don't like it, Almeida is I fear, a rogue and Clark the *experto*[89] has allowed himself to be done by him.

Sunday, 24th November

All alone the others on leave. Wet morning, have got cold, said on board all day. Serious thoughts of sending for my Father and family.

Saturday, 30th November

Most of this week has been wet (light rain) but today is fine being on holiday, appointed such by the Governor of the state as a day of thanksgiving for the admission of this place as a state. I went to the Mission, took my gun, saw several wild ducks and 5 golden Plover, shot one of the latter. In 48 hours of this week, 53 vessels entered, one of them a French vessel brought 50 women, Ladies.

Sunday, 1st December

Closed my No. 78 to Liz promising to write to my Father by next Packet, none of hers to answer. The sun is out but the air is cold.

Monday, 9th December

The weather has continued mild and fine with the exception of a few occasional showers. Today by packet received Eliza's No. 92, closed 24th Sept. 1850. She had received my No. 69 closed 15th July 1850. Also received letters from Liot dated London 15th October 1850 and from M.E. Rawes from Heaton Mersey, near Manchester, 11th October 1850. She is in England putting the girls to school, my Ma and my 2 sisters had left for Porto and she. Mr. E.R. would follow next month. Our houses received encouraging letters from Portugal, Garland, Laidley & Co. hold out hopes of consignments from Lisbon.

---

[89] Wise-guy, "clever" one

Friday, 13ᵗʰ December

At 1:30 P.M. the first lashing of the Cordonasso[90] visited us, raising a sea that tossed the boats, us even with the ships bulwarks and blowing great guns from all parts of the compass accompanied with rain. The *Braemar* of Calcutta, a barque, ran into us and set her Cat. Head through our bulwarks and carried three of the fore stanchions. It abated about 4:30 P.M. after doing much damage amongst the shipping; a sloop near us had to throw all her cargo overboard.

Saturday, 14ᵗʰ December

At 9 P.M. a fire broke out in the block between Montgomery California and Sacramento streets, consuming it nearly all; the fire engines of which not less than 20 were present, worked admirable and by their efforts, prevented its spreading. We got a fright it being near the office; I cleared out and got to the boat and set the things on board by 11:30 it was plain that the fire would not spread more so I took our papers onshore for Clark to finish his Packet.

Sunday, 15ᵗʰ December

The site of the fire is still smouldering. It commenced in a new building and is supposed to have been the work of incendiaries.

Closed and posted my No. 79 to Liz, and a letter to my Father, with my advice as to his coming out here or not. Weather yesterday and today fine, mild but gloomy.

---

[90] Cordonasso/Cardonasso/Cardonasse. Probably the local name for one of the strong winter winds that can assail San Francisco, although I could find no reference to any name similar to the one used by HEW. "California can receive a deluge of precipitation when significant subtropical moisture makes its way across the Pacific and interacts with a West Coast trough. Meteorologists often dub this occurrence "the Pineapple Express." Source: Storm Encyclopedia – Winter Storms – Pacific: http://www.weather.com/encyclopedia/winter/pacific. html. I wonder if this is not a variant of "Coronados", i.e. a wind that comes from the direction of the Coronados Islands near San Francisco?

I yesterday made complaint at the Harbourmaster's office about the damage done us by the *Braemer*. Took another office in Gibb's house, along with a room upstairs, these two being taken along with N.P. Mackay, being a land agent, does not interfere with our business.

Wednesday, 18th December

Last week I hired our launch to the *Braemer* to drop her anchor for $10.00. Today I have Ben bring in her a load of goods onboard to store on Gibb's account for which we get $4.00 per ton for lightering on board and storing for one month, being $2.00 for lightering and $2.00 for storing. A lot of his goods also came in a scow (which scow is the largest I ever saw, said to carry 70 tons) to store on his account. On the 14th, I was sent one doz. shirts at $.00 per doz.! very cheap! the usual price being $8.00.

* * *

The weather has continued fine with the exception of a shower of rain, and fog yesterday, but the former showed us we must get the decks caulked, as the wet came through to the cargo, so we sent for Mr. Van Duren to do it. Also found out today where the ship leaks, by taking out a lining board from the starboard side, and found the water gurgling in by the side of a nail in a stream as thick as a quill.

Thursday, 19th December

Gave the ship a list to larboard so as to lift two sheets of copper out of water, then Van drove the nail out and put a trunnel in its place; she now makes only water enough to keep her sweet.

Saturday, 21st December

Saw a very large bear on shore, shot up the river, as fast as possible. I have called several times this week on the harbourmaster without being able to see him, he being out, but spoke to him today and he promised to come at 2 o'clock and see to the damage, but has not been. More cargo came on board to store, belonging to Green.

* * *

I bought a small launch about 4-5 tons off a Mr. Henry Fligg, passenger, from on board the *Braemer*. She is built of Sidney, hard wood, very strong. I gave $50.00 for her and consider I got her for half her value. This Mr. Fligg, is a Yorkshire Man, knows John Lord in Sidney and had seen Toni Chaster there, is going there in a short time and offers to take letters to Toni.

Sunday, 22ⁿᵈ December
Laidley and José gone shooting. I went to the Congregational Church[91] and heard an excellent discourse relative to keeping the Sabbath holy, and after shewing that this place being in its infancy, strenuous effort ought to be made to establish from the first, proper observance of it, also alluding to the Packets sometimes leaving on Sundays and on the way to Church, I saw lots of placards announcing a grand masked ball for tonight, this evening; others equally large are posted over them saying the ball is postponed till tomorrow night and our fellow citizens are requested to attend, that the proprietor may find he is no looser by ceding to the request of some friends to desist from such entertainment on the Sabbath!

Wednesday, 25ᵗʰ December
We have had the weather beautiful since the first visit of the Cordonasso, clear sky, warm and today is really beautiful. I have had a very long walk down to the seashore outside the bar, where for the first time, shot an eagle and 2 ducks; saw 7 eagles, one shot dead by

---

[91] First Congregational Church, corner of Jackson and Virginia sts., Rev. T. D. Hunt, h. corner of Mason and Vallejo sts.

a Frenchman, the one I shot fell down a precipice where I could not get it.

On the cliffs overlooking the sea I discussed the contents of my haversack, how I enjoyed the lonely repast! That finished, nature's book before me, pointed to its author! Can anyone in or out of church be more struck by their presence there, amongst others, than alone on the cliffs where the eagle soars the broad and angry sea before and the forest around there unfettered by the presence of man, the closeness of the pew and may not the knee bend on the green sod, and a prayer be offered up as fervent as ever passed the lips of man? Let those who ever felt such moments answer. Last night I was at the circus, good Chinese dance.

Thursday, 26th December

We have the launch turned up alongside, and Van is caulking her; today I struck the foretopmast so as to get the ship snug for winter. At 8 P.M. we heard the fire bell going on shore, passed the alarm with our bell then went ashore with our launch. The fire was at the top of Broadway on the hill, the engines were at work passing water one to another all the way from the Polka deposit to the fire and another line from the north beach at least one mile distant, still the fire was seen got under; it had taken in some hay and lumber which was burnt, value bout $10,000.00[92]

Friday, 27th December

The Packet due 22nd has not yet appeared and fears are entertained for her as several vessels have come in severely damaged by the Cordonasso of the 18th instant and news has arrived of several vessels having been picked up dismasted in various parts of the Pacific. A whaler from this port was struck by a sea and soon after floundered. The Captain and 6 men saved themselves in a whaleboat and got safe back here.

---

[92] The main Parker House gambling casino burnt down to the ground.

Saturday, 28th December

Blew a N.E. gale in the night but no harm done, beautiful day and clear night, sun very warm. A steamer entered from Panama, sailed 48 hours after the Packet which brought the mail, but has heard nothing of her.

Tuesday, 31st December

Weather has been very pleasant, clear, warm and dry. As I am going over to the other side of the Bay tomorrow shooting, I closed and handed to Clark to post my No. 80 to Liz, complaining of not having heard from her for so long.

San Francisco Bay - 1st January 1851, Wednesday

In the morning, left the ship in the little Fairy with Senhor José and António for the contracosta, very foggy soon after we left but having a pocket compass, steered by it; about midday pulling, there being no wind, we fell in with a boat, about 7 tons, with two Chileans, Don Jose Manuel Calleja and a friend bound to Temascal. They were becalmed and had lost their way so they invited us to join them and accompany them home when the fog should clear, so we tied our boat astern of theirs and plied their oars till we grounded. Our friends being convinced we were close to their house, induced us to go ahead in the small boat till she grounded, then to jump out and walk to their house to send horses for them.

We went some distance when the Fairy grounded, we then jumped out, ankle deep in mud and water and walked to the shore about ½ a mile, the beach on the other side being almost flat for near three miles, below high water mark. The fog was very thick so we had to leave one of the party now, and then on our track and keep shouting to prevent our loosing the direction of the boats.

I lead the way with compass in one hand and boat hook in the other and a hatchet in my belt; the mud is not deep in any place on the contracosta and I got on well amidst thousands of wild fowl, I startled two beautiful swans amongst them. I at last reached the shore, but found nothing but brush-weed, no signs of habitation, night coming on. I hastened back to the boats, as the tide came in, we all walked on board the big boat, I changed my boots, they being the shooting boots, had not let in water. We then made a fire, had tea and some preserved meats I had with me and went to sleep in the covered boat; I had plenty of clothes and slept well.

Thursday, 2ⁿᵈ January

Very foggy, cleared a little at 10, when we got onshore and found ourselves near San Leandro, amidst thousands of wild ducks and geese, but being anxious to get to our friends' house for rest and a full belly, we shoved off and came down the coat, but about a league above Temascal the large boat grounded, two miles from shore. We all took to the small one, went on a mile when it grounded; we anchored it and all got out to walk.

After walking a mile in water we found a deep channel preventing our getting on shore so had to return to the big boat as night was coming on again and the tide also filling might have caught us on this bank; we got on board her, very tired, I changed clothes, lit fire, had tea and another tin of preserved meat, then laid down till morning.

Friday, 3ʳᵈ January

Morning foggy, no land to be seen but we knew our course and pulled the large boat in search of the Fairy, but in vain, the fog was so thick we could not see her, so steered for the Temascal where we arrived safe and were well treated by our host who sent his men for my boat whilst we rested. The fog continued too thick to start, so in the evening our host gave us a first rate entertainment, first rate table, French cook, sweet wine. Hock, Champagne, sweetmeats, coffee and excellent company.

Towards evening, fog on shore cleared off a little and we had a fine view of the beautiful green plain on which we were, nothing was wanting for a most eligible farm; cattle innumerable, were grazing about. The plain is principally inhabited by Chileans.

Saturday, 4th January

Left Temascal in company of Sr. Calleja in his boat towing ours for town, clear fine day. When I got here found as I expected all in alarm at my absence. Clark had just arranged a boat commanded by Moniz who was to take a three-day trip in search of me. The Papers had mentioned our absence. Laidley said he was worn out with fatigue and anxiety being constantly on the lookout for us. The missing steamer had arrived, but no letters for me.

Wednesday, 15th January

Closed No. 81 for Liz but an old Steamer, the *Unicorn* being laid on for the mail, few people liking to write by her, preferring writing by the *Tennessee*[93] to sail on the 23rd so I followed the stream and postponed posting it. Aubrey had arranged to go by this Packet to England, thence to Porto and Lisbon, but resolved to remain for the *Tennessee*; he had offered to take a parcel for me which I prepared, a map of San Francisco in 1849 and 50 views of same at different eras, some ribbons for Sisters, a China shawl or handkerchief for Liz, and a print of the admission from Clark for Mr. Rawes, to whom not addressed the parcel as my Father would not be in town to see to it. I gave Aubrey a letter of introduction to Uncle John.

---

[93] Wooden side-wheel steamer, 2 decks, 3 masts. Accommodations for 200, enlarged in 1849 to carry 200 cabin and 350 steerage. The SS Tennessee was initially to run weekly service between New York and Savannah, but she was bought by Howland & Aspinwall/Pacific Mail Steamship Company for the California trade. The Tennessee was the first American steamship whose service was interrupted to be used in the Panama run. She was provisioned for a Pacific voyage by way of the Straits of Magellan and on her first run, because of storms, she carried only 15 passenger, passing the equator on December 23, 1849.

When she reached Panama on March 12, 1850 after 57 days at sea from New York, she was met by 3,000 people waiting forpassage to San Francisco. She brought thousands of gold-seekers to the City before sinking just outside of San Francisco's fog-shrouded headlands on March 6, 1853 in an area which is now named Tennessee Cove in her honor. Her passengers, mail and baggage were saved, but she was a total loss.

Sunday, 19ᵗʰ January

I went to the opening of the new Presbyterian Church[94] in Stockton Street, found it crowded to the door, went to another, also crowded, and at last found room to sit in a third and heard an excellent sermon. The town very gay today, wharf full of Ladies walking out. We have beautiful weather, could not be more pleasant.

Tuesday, 21ˢᵗ January

Received from Packet, two letters from Liz and one from Ma. Liz's No. 93 and 95, the former dated 14ᵗʰ October, closed 22ⁿᵈ October, acknowledging receipt of my No. 70 of 27ᵗʰ to 31ˢᵗ July which she received 7ᵗʰ October, notices on the 21ˢᵗ October, this night twelve months we parted. Taits are kind to her, sending her news of us when they get any, lump no larger[95], says the papers talk of a new route being opened by Nicaragua instead of Panama, gives a copy of her letter to John, "good".

No 95 dated 11ᵗʰ closed 15ᵗʰ November, had received on the 4ᵗʰ November, my No. 72 of 31ˢᵗ August and in it the gold dollar I sent her, will obey orders to write twice a month, Packets leave Lisbon 3 times a month, 9ᵗʰ, 19ᵗʰ and 29ᵗʰ and leave for Chagres only 2 each month. Sophy's[96] remarks about the small importance of our letters compared with Garland, Laidley and Co's. Liz tifted[97] at it and gives her a spirited answer, is a plucky girl. Hers of 31ˢᵗ October (I suppose No. 94) she forwarded to my Father to send to me (it had not come to hand).

The 12ᵗʰ November was one year since I left Lisbon. She has bought a monkey like the one I had, she is taking riding lessons to

---

[94] First Presbyterian Church, Superior Court Room City Hall, Rev. A. Williams, home Dupont st. between Broadway and Pacific sts. Worship on Sundays at 11 o'clock A. M., and 4 and 7 1-2 o'clock P. M. (This was the address of the church after it was rebuilt following its destruction by fire later that year.)

[95] Would this be the "bad news" from Eliza that HEW refers to earlier?

[96] Sophia Laidley, John Searle's fiancée.

[97] An interesting verb based on the expression "in a tiff", i.e., to be annoyed.

please me, George[98] also taking them, I suppose to please her, there is a circus in Fig.[99] lump same, has a light cold.

The letter I received from Ma, dated Lisbon 17th October 1850, she has been down to Sintra[100] with Leonora and Sarah Alice and will take the first steamer for Porto. Jim Garland's note to John casts a slur on Clark and I, caused I suppose by some remarks of John's.

Thursday, 23rd January
Closed and posted my No. 82 with No. 81 in it as it did not go by the mail. I also wrote to my Father, Aunt Elizabeth, and John Searle giving him a rap about Jim's letter. Aubrey went by the *Tennessee* today and took my parcel for home.

Friday, 24th January
A little rain fell in the night, but the day is clear again, we catch lots of crabs alongside. Plenty of nice *Sardinhas*[101] selling about.

Sunday, 26th January
Yesterday and today had a diarrhoea *de sangue e matteria*[102], took plenty of barley water and arrowroot, abstaining from other food.

Monday, 27th January
All right again, at a loss how to account for it except it be from some bad water I drank on board the *May Mitchell* when I went for the barley and beans.

Friday, 31st January
The weather had been rather thick lately and once or twice a little rain at night. I dined at Gibb's, then went with Clark for a walk through

---

[98] George Searle, brother to Eliza.
[99] Figueira da Foz.
[100] Near Lisbon.
[101] Sardines
[102] Blood and faeces

the gambling houses; they were rather thinly attended and a little betting going on. In one storey of the Parker House[103] were two new paintings of naked women, full size, in the most indelicate positions. Every one reproved the power that their senses have over sense, thence we went up and sat for an hour at Castre's, where I received a present of a Chinese feather fan from Dona Joanita for one to send to Portugal.

The Indians have been fighting the whites up the country and volunteers are paid $8.00 per day and feed, to go and fight them.

Saturday, 1st February

Closed and posted my No. 83 to Liz, giving her copy of extract of my letter to John by last Packet. Wrote to Aunt Jane[104] and to Uncle John, enclosing the other two letters, both in mine to Uncle. I told him that before this I supposed he would have handed to him by Mr. Rawes, 263 pounds about, on account, of the bills and after we sell our barley and beans, shall remit the rest.

Sunday, 2nd February

Went to Church at the new Presbyterian Church, and partook of the Lord's Supper[105] for the first time in California, all forms are dispensed with by this church. I was not prepared, that is I had a week's

---

[103] Located on Portsmouth Square. «On the east side, a contemporary tells us, there was in September, 1850, "a line of palaces, the magnificence of whose interior even more than corresponds to the promise as their outward show. They were all devoted to the fickle goddess, Fortune, but they are good lounges for one who can withstand temptation." At the right was the three-storied El Dorado, a fireproof building that had saved some of its weaker neighbors during the last conflagration. It was a favorite resort of the Mexican gamblers. Next stood the Parker House, the third of its name on the same site. The first was built in the spring of 1849 by Robert A. Parker and John H. Brown. It fronted sixty-five feet on the plaza and was 145 feet deep, with a wing thirty-five feet wide running back ninety feet. The whole structure was two stories high...» Source: San Francisco City History website.

[104] Jane Emma Wilby m. George CHASTER, sister to Ann Wilby, HEW's mother.

[105] Communion. The forms HEW refers to are prior confession and fasting.

preparation, but felt that in turning my back to such an invite I should but prove myself of the name of a Christian, for how can a man turn his back on such a celebration when he thinks "This night I may die and shall I refuse to obey the command of him who died to redeem me from sin".

The address given by the preacher was touching in the extreme, and let those sneer who are ashamed to own their Master. I felt afraid lest I should be presuming too much, but at the same time an irresistible inclination to stay and be one of the flock who mind the Shepherd's call. Suffice it that I felt assured my duty was to stay, as also a voice within me told me such was a privilege I have not forfeited.

Friday, 7ᵗʰ February

Spent the evening on board the *Braemer*.

Saturday, 8ᵗʰ February

Yesterday and today some heavy showers of rain have fallen, which have done much good. I received a letter from Bannister, from the mines.

Sunday, 9ᵗʰ February

Beautiful day, folks wearing white trousers. It has rained well up the country for a day or two. Clark and Laidley went to a picnic at the lake (where I also was invited, but would not go, being better engaged). They got into a row there and the hilarity of the party was somewhat dampened by blows. I passed the day better for my taste, went to church twice, morning and evening, the latter at 7 o'clock.

Monday, 10ᵗʰ February

Had a visit from Abreu, Captain of the barque *Lydia*. Bought some seed for my bird at $1.00 per lb. The *California* Panama Packet has not appeared yet, though she ought to have been here at the beginning of the month.

Saturday, 15th February

Closed and posted my No. 84 to Liz under cover to Prescott Bro. & Co. and enclosed in it my first letter to George Searle. I mentioned that the *Constitution* had arrived with the *California's* mails, but had not yet got my letters.

Sunday, 16th February

Received the following letters, No. 94 from Liz, closed 31st October 1850, all well. Also 2 letters from my Father, one dated Vizella 26th August 1850, the other 14th November 1850; he wants to come out here alone. Also a letter from Sarah Wilby from London, 20th September 1850. Also letter from Lavinia and Leonora, Vizella 20th November 1850.

The house received a letter for John Searle from Jim Garland dated 30th November which tells John by no means to return as his leaving would be ruination to the house. *Arre Arre.*[106] Received orders to see after a consignment sent to Gunter and Brooks.

Monday, 17th February

On Saturday last, after scrubbing the cabin with sand, Laidley came into it and picked up several bits of gold; we then proceeded to wash the sand remaining in the bucket, and found it to contain a lot of black sand in which was a good deal of very fine gold dust, but scarcely enough to be worth the trouble of washing it. The sand was brought down from the foot of that heap of sand near the iron foundry, Happy Valley.

Tuesday, 18th February

A good shower of rain fell followed by a strong land wind, there was a terrible gale of wind, on this coast on the 14th instant, worse than any hitherto seen, two steamers hence for Trinity put back. 4 lots of

---

[106] Yeah, yeah!

fine mussels, $1.00 a 100, 4 inches long, lots of crabs selling at .50 per doz., 4 inches broad.

Friday, 28th February

The Packet for Panama is postponed till the 5th approx. March. Weather fine but rather cold.

Sunday, 2nd March

José Corte Real picked up a small oak built boat, waterlogged.

Monday, 3rd March

This morning at 2 o'clock, the steamer *S. Clara* took fire alongside long wharf and was burnt nearly to the water's edge. 3 men were burnt to death in her; the flames spread to the steamer *Hartford*, which was also half burnt, the remainder of her being saved by the exertions of the fire companies which were seen at work with their engines. It was a grand though awful sight; crowds of boats were round the burning vessels; fears were entertained that the flames might pass to other vessels but luckily they were prevented from so doing. At 9 A.M. both the steamers were towed up to Happy Valley, still smouldering, to be built up again.

Tuesday, 4th March

This morning about 3 A.M. a fire broke out, south of Pine Street behind Macondray's and swept away a good number of houses. When it began the wind was very strong off shore and I was afraid the sparks which were coming over this way might set our ship on fire, so got all ready to let go the chains and haul her out of danger. When we were just ready to let go the chains, the wind abated and the fire was got under by the exertions of the firemen. Had the wind continued the whole or greater part of the city must have been burnt and perhaps the shipping. I went on shore to see the fires, mostly small houses burnt.

Wednesday, 5th March

Closed and posted my No. 85 for Liz at 11 A.M. At 5 P.M. we got the Packet letters but none from Liz, one letter only from Tait with invoice of milk, punch and Boots per *Desire* and a private letter from W.G. Roughten to Clark. There being little to do, I am preparing for a trip to the contracosta morrow to spend a few days.

Thursday, 6th March

After dinner in the small launch with António and with a fair wind aft, arrived in about an hour and a half at Temascal. I had all arranged for sleeping in the boat, but Canilha, Calhias' partner, would not allow me to do so, and arranged me a bed of bear skins (first rate) and had all my things taken to his house. Calhias was absent, at San Francisco.

Friday, 7th March

Canilha caught a horse for me and off I went on it. Shooting, Antonio accompanying me on foot, we rode up the valley behind the rancho, behind the hills by the fir trees and thence down to the beach back to the house. In a rivulet near the fir trees we caught 2 fine trout by hand. It is a most beautiful valley or *corgo*[107]; the fir trees are very high, straight and free from knots, good for masts, like our *Pinho Manso*[108], some 3 feet in diameter and very long.

I saw two coveys of partridges but very wild; chased a wolf but the scamp at a canter, beat my nag at full speed. I shot a wild goose of which there are thousands about but unapproachable except on horseback.

Saturday, 8th March

Canilha again by the use of his lasso furnished me with a nag, we brought in three cows, tied their legs, milked them, a good fill of milk, then I started with António northward along the plain almost as far as

---

[107] Portuguese for river valley.
[108] Mediterranean or stone pine

the entrance of the Sacramento. The plain in beautiful for agricultural purposes and covered with cattle, but best about the Temascal; the rest appears too damp and marshy.

I shot three wild geese by getting near the flock on horseback and when they are ready to fly, gallop up to them and let drive for they have been too much hunted to let you approach near enough for a good shot. Calhega arrived in the afternoon.

*   *   *

In the evening I was taken to a Ball at the rancho by Canilha. It was much better than I could have expected, a large and well furnished room contained about 50 men and 16 nice young ladies, Californians. At the end of the room sat in state the acting *majordomo*[109], *brother to the dono do rancho*[110] who was absent. He was a fine portly looking man of about 70, has a father alive, 120 years old and his brother 80, being owner of a large rancho further up the plain. His daughter was the belle of the room; a delicate shape, fair complexion and pretty feet made her the *punto central de belleza*[111]. Two Indians played the guitar to dance to and during the evening were dances, quadrilles, *francezas*[112], waltzes, polkas, *contradança inglesa*[113], *contradança California*[114] - something like the English Contradança and the *gota*[115] - and an Indian shuffle.

Sunday, 9th March

Mass was said at the rancho; upwards of 40 young California Ladies attended, some from a distance came in carts. After this ceremony, two Indians were baptised one 9 and the other 11 years

---

[109] Estate manager/steward
[110] Owner of the estate
[111] centre of attention
[112] French-style quadrilles
[113] Eightsome reels
[114] Square dancing
[115] Gavotte

old. The females called Californias are Spaniards (the copper coloured natives being called Indian) are generally very fair and pretty. The owner of the rancho sports his comfortable English carriage.

When I was here before, Calhega was enclosing a parcel of land and [*sic.*]going to sew it. It is now sewn and the blades of barley up; he has sewn a large piece with barley and about 300 pounds of potatoes and if they turn out well will make a fortune. My friends pressed me to stay but fearing bad weather, I left at 2 P.M. but having head wind did not get here till 8 P.M. found all right on board.

Saturday, 15ᵗʰ March

Closed and posted my No. 86 for Liz, also gave Clark a letter for Lavinia to enclose to Mr. Rawes.

Tuesday, 18ᵗʰ March

Abreu, Captain of *Lydia* got knocked down on long wharf by one of his sailors that had come out with him, others pinioned him as that he could not return the blow and he had to take refuge in a restaurant. The steamer *Hartford* that was half burnt down on the 3ʳᵈ passed out here ready to resume her work, busy painting. Wet evening. I wrote to Bannister at Wood's diggings.

Wednesday, 19ᵗʰ March

Last night and this morning it rained pretty heavily, this morning we had some hail. Cold and windy, midday fine. I this morning bought of José his share of the boat he picked up for $16.00, the notice in the Picayune stipulated 10 days for her being claimed in and that time having elapsed. Bannister arrived from the mines for a few days and gave me a specimen of gold.

Friday, 21ˢᵗ March

Clark went off to Sacramento City with Mr. and Mrs. Castro purporting to be back in Monday or Tuesday.

Saturday, 22nd March

Received from Packet a letter from my Father of Vizella 2nd December announcing death of Baby on 23rd November 1850. One from John Wilby of 7th December with Liz's No. 96 in it. An envelope with Liz's No. 97 and a letter for Laidley in it. A letter from Jane Chaster[116] in it, Liz's No. 98, closed 24th December 1850. John Searle had arrived in Porto 22nd December and also a letter from John Wilby, one from Carr and from Roughton, all to the house, the latter covering Bills of Lading for wine and from *Desire* and John Wilby's mention of goods he is shipping from London.

António Ruina (our Cook) settled accounts with me today as he is going to the mines tomorrow. He left with me $300.00 and 2½ ounces of gold to take care of. Yesterday 21st, I agreed and brought on board Henry Hogan to serve as cook at $30.00 a month, recommended by Mackay.

Sunday, 23rd March

Received an *Officio*[117] from the Health Office of Portugal with the health regulations. Was late at church.

Monday, 24th March

Spent the evening with Mrs. Gardiner at Mrs. Hodson's. Bannister boards there also, along with several Skipperesses. Was introduced to Mrs. Creifey, Mrs. Rattery, Mrs. Fouchee, whose husbands are at gold bluff, and 2 Misses Thomson whose husbands are yet in the inkstand. Bannister aspires to the honour of bearing that title of affinity to the sulky one. Also introduced to Peter, a rum chap, the fun of the house, and Captain Evans of the brig *Prospect*. Spent pleasant evening, Gardiner is at Gold Bluffs.

[116] Jane Emma Wilby Chaster, HEW's Aunt Jane.
[117] Official letter, notice

Sunday, 30ᵗʰ March

Clark arrived from Sacramento, no news, very reserved.

Monday, 31ˢᵗ March

Ever since the 8 or 9ᵗʰ we have had rain nearly every day, though about midday it is usually fine; we have had several storms, pretty heavy on the coast.

Tuesday, 1ˢᵗ April

Closed my No. 87 to Liz and enclosed it along with one to my Father in one to Uncle John sent per *Tennessee* to the care of S.B. Carr. I also wrote to Uncle John in the name of the House. No. 87 was received by Liz 9ᵗʰ June 1851.

* * *

Copy of a recipe given me by George Searle, for making blue writing ink:

> ½ oz powdered Prussian blue
> ½ oz powdered oxalic acid
> 1 pint distilled water
> The blue and the acid are to be put into a bottle with cold water and well shaken as often as may be convenient for two or three days.

Sunday, 6ᵗʰ April

Received per Packet two letters, one from Lavinia, 16ᵗʰ December 1850 Porto and one from Mrs. Rawes Porto 27ᵗʰ January 1851.

Tuesday, 15ᵗʰ April

Closed and posted my No. 88 to Liz and wrote to Jane Chaster enclosing my letter to Liz in it and sent to the care of Carr. No. 88 was received 16ᵗʰ June 1851.

Thursday, 24th April

In the morning, called on Boyd on board his schooner *Wanderer* and was much amused with my visit. He has a collection of all kinds of curiosities collected in the course of his voyages - Indian armour, war implements - and he has been in Portugal and Spain and is now concerned in a gold digging company of the quartz rocks at Woods diggings. We set our names down in the visitors' books where he has the signatures of many Indian Chieftains with their *rubrica*[118] (*como a de um tabellião*[119])-

In the afternoon got our Packet letters. I received from Liz her No. 99 dated from 26th December to 4th January 1851. No. 100, 8th January to 14th January 1851. A P.S. to No. 100, 23rd and 24th January 1851 and No. 1 of a new hundred, 20th January to 15th February 1851. My Nos. 74, 75, 76, 77, 78, the latter closed here 1st December 1851.

Also received a letter from my Father dated Vizella 6th January 1851 and plenty of business letters with letters from John Searle.

Thursday, 1st May

Closed and posted my No. 89 to Liz, sent it along with a letter to my Father enclosed in a business letter to my Uncle John, remitting my Uncle our Draft at 3 days for 320 pounds, and also remitted my Father $50.00 to be paid him by Mr. Rawes. Also enclosed a letter for José de Campos dated 28th April.

Sunday, 4th May

Last night at 11:30 P.M. a fire broke out in the plaza, the wind increasing to a gale, it swept, despite the exertions of the firemen, in all directions, as far as Pine St., south, Dupont West, beyond Pacific St. North and East down nearly to the end of the wharf, burning up nearly everything within these boundaries; many brick buildings considered fireproof were reduced to ashes. Gibb's, Argentes and some

---

[118] mark
[119] Like that of a notary's, i.e., like a seal

others escaped; four store ships blocked in high and dry were burnt, viz. *Niantic, General Harrison, Apollo* and another.

The sparks flew over the shipping away to the island, some of the vessels had their sails set on fire, but were put out, all being on the lookout. I slipped our chains and laid on warps ready to haul out. I brought our books and papers and cash off on board; the fire still rages, but (at 10 P.M. Sunday) its further progress is stopped.

Monday, 5ᵗʰ May

Fire still rages, consuming the remains of the buildings in its power yesterday. This evening I saw Clark for the first time since the fire, he having slept on board of some ship, although he promised to come off and help to haul out the ship if requisite. We, that is, Laidley, the boy and I, had to clear the ship for hauling out, slip the chains, lay out warps, wet the decks and finally to heave in our chains again. I quite knocked up, with the work and anxiety and having got my hands singed in the fire on Sunday morning, they are yet painful.

Tuesday, 6ᵗʰ May

The *Northerner* Packet arrived this morning, but did not bring the British mail. Laidley and I went on board her expecting Searle, but he did not come. On shore things are looking up again, for many of the safes were opened today and found to contain all the cash of the bankers and principal merchants untouched, so these are setting to work to build again. Many went off to the mines yesterday and today, but more are busy at work removing the ruins and buildings. 15 bodies have been found burnt and doubtless many more are burnt. Men are getting $1.50 per hour to clear away the rubbish and have refused $200.00 per month to ship. It bids fair to have the city rebuilt in a very short time.

Wednesday, 7ᵗʰ May

The city of Stockton was yesterday nearly all destroyed by fire, the work of incendiaries beyond a doubt.

Monday, 12ᵗʰ May

Wrote a private letter to Uncle John with a full account of the fire and desired him to let our folks know we are all well. In it I enclosed my No. 90 to Liz closed this morning and sent it through Carr per the Express Steamer *Carolina*, which leaves today.

Thursday, 15ᵗʰ May

Closed and posted my No. 91 to Liz, enclosed in a business letter to Uncle John. I closed it at 10 A.M. but had not then heard of the earthquake[120] which was felt here this morning at 8 A.M. The shock was felt on shore very severe and also felt on board the vessels, though I did not feel it. Laidley said he did, but did not say so till after I told him of it.

Sunday, 18ᵗʰ May

Last night the barometer fell to 29.8, thermometer 58, blowing strong, and during the night it rained very hard. This morning at 10 A.M. the barometer up 29.9, thermometer 60. At midday it cleared up a little. It is a very extraordinary thing to have rain at this time of the year.

Tuesday, 20ᵗʰ May

John Searle arrived here again from Portugal. He brought me Liz's No. 2 dated Figueira 30ᵗʰ and 31ˢᵗ January 1851, also a pair of slippers sent by her for me. A book sent me by Lavinia, a letter from Leonora, Sarah Alice and Louisa viz. 13ᵗʰ January, one from Wm. Wilby, viz. 4ᵗʰ February and one from John Wilby 18ᵗʰ February. I had been on board the steamer *Tennessee* to meet him but he had left before I got there.

---

[120] Earthquake records became more accurate with the arrival of Thomas Tennant in San Francisco during the Gold Rush. He kept weather observations and noted local earthquakes.

Saturday, 31st May

Closed and posted my No. 92 to Liz. Presented my diploma[121] to Butler King, Collector, along with Searle, he was very civil.

Sunday, 1st June

Two years today since I last arrived in Porto from Figueira with Eliza and John. Went to church with John and Laidley to Dr. Ver Mehr's Church[122], did not like the sermon. *Princess Royal* arrived with the first goods consigned to us.

Tuesday, 3rd June

Received per Packet the following letters from Liz. No 3 and its P.S. and No. 4 and 5 and a letter from L.A.[123] Wilby dated Porto 14th March, the P.S. to No. 3 brought an olive leaf enclosed (*Paz?*[124]).

Sunday, 8th June

At church (Presb.) morning and evening; in evening the sermon was about the present state and future prospects of the Jews.

Monday, 9th June

At 3 p.m. went over with Searle to Angel Island in the Fairy, slept there in a tent we rigged on the shore.

Tuesday, 10th June

Set sail again from Angel Island early and got here about 10 A.M. having taken one hour and ten minutes to come over in the Fairy. Met Manuel Gallego on long wharf; has been to Sydney.

---

[121] Presumably, the ship's documents, as the "Collector" was responsible for all taxes and internal revenue in San Francisco. Vessels that violated the Federal revenue laws were seized.

[122] Grace Chapel, Powell Street, Rev. P. L. Ver Mehr, home corner of Jackson and Powell Streets.

[123] Lavinia Anne Wilby, presumably.

[124] Peace. This was again a period of considerable political unrest in Portugal.

Hanging of John Jenkins[125]

Last night at 11 o'clock, the Private Police caught a man in the act of getting off in a boat with a small safe containing $200.00. They tried him, found him guilty and sentenced him to be hung, which sentence was carried into effect at 1 o'clock this morning by the people. This example will or ought to strike terror into the hearts of the malefactors who infest this city! His name was Simpt(s)on of London, alias Jenkins (here). He had been transported from London for Arson and Murder and had lately arrived here from Sidney. It has caused great excitement in town.

---

[125] «This drawing represents the outcome of the first trial and sentence of a criminal by indignant citizens who took the law into their own hands to suppress the crimes that flooded the state. The courts were apparently in the hands of the politicians and riffraff of the city, who used the processes of the law for their own profit. There were many murders between 1849 and 1851, but the perpetrators readily escaped punishment and hangings were rare. The ballot box and the city administration of justice was a farce. The indignation of the better class of citizens was at fever heat. On June 9, 1851, at Sydney cove, John Jenkins walked deliberately into a merchants store, picked up the small safe, carried it to a boat at a nearby wharf and coolly rowed out into the bay. The alarm was given, and a number of merchants pursued an overtook the man. He threw the safe overboard. Jenkins was brought back and taken to a building that occupied a corner at Sansome and Pine streets, the site on which the Royal Insurance Building is now located. The prisoner duly tried by a jury and condemned to be hanged. The impromptu Vigilance Committee wasted no time, and the execution took place in the Plaza the same night at 2 a.m. This prompt action had its effect on the criminal class, and for a while they remained under cover.» In: *San Francisco News Letter* September 1925

END OF A PARTNERSHIP

Thursday, 12th June

Went to try our Rifles up Mission Creek. Laidley wounded a polecat and got served out by its spitting in his eyes; I settled its hash with a rifle bullet.

Friday, 13th June

One year today since we arrived here! Today I brought on board the first part of the cargo ex. *Princess Royal*, the first consignment we have received. The day was wound up as such festive days but too often are! In the evening a quarrel took place in which Clark being blamed for having sold some wine on credit, he retaliated saying that Searle had no business to endorse the Bill for Rawes, and hot words ensued, John promising to inform his Uncle.

Saturday, 14th June

John wrote to Rawes stating Clark's conduct and telling him to expect that our partnership would not continue, also saying that I concurred. In all he said, I wrote to my Father to the same effect. In my letter to my Dad, I wrote a few hints about my marriage and I enclosed it for perusal and to be forwarded to Liz in my No. 93 of 17 pages! to her.

Sunday, 15th June

Sunday, at Church in the morning, on board the rest of the day, evening damp and unpleasant.

Monday, 16th June

Our worst fears confirmed with regard to Clark. Many accounts known to us as received not appearing in his book as received, and on being questioned about them said he did not know it was that they were missing, although one item was $300.00.

Searle and I brought books on board and examined them to ascertain the amounts received by him and not accounted for. My feelings as the truth gradually became more visible, were distressing in the extreme. We were up till after 12 P.M. at work on these accounts.

Tuesday, 17*th* June

The events of this day will be long graven deep on my mind, for my hand trembles and my nerves are unstrung by them. I have seen one respected as a friend and trusted as one of us stand in the light of a crime, one haughty proud of himself and one who has ill treated me, writhing in the most abject state of misery and remorse and begging for my mercy at my hands; a heart of stone could not have looked on the scene unmoved oh! horrible!

Searle and I, though both resolved to carry matters to extremes (which for our safety was necessary) were both moved. I could not contain my tears to witness the humiliating state to which his actions have reduced him (an American woman of the town has been the cause of his ruin) and from the determinations to press the matter, we find ourselves resolving to accept his premises of amendment, hoping this will be a lesson to him. Also we were pretty sure that if we pressed it, he, to escape the infamy, must cut short a life unbearable.

This, some would say should be buried in oblivion, but I say no! for no one knows to what they may be tempted and perhaps this being kept fresh in my mind may deter me from ever doing anything of which I may be ashamed and may God grant it may be the means of commencing the work of reformation in him who brought this lesson at so dear a price, is my sincere prayer.

Thursday, 19*th* June

Clark wrote a letter to Searle and me asking to be allowed to continue till the end of our term in Partnership to which we consented, hoping he had had lesson enough.

Friday, 20th June

Received from Packet the following letters: of Eliza No. 16 Porto 3rd to 7th April 1851. Sarah Wilby *viz.* 14th March 1851 and three from William Wilby, Porto 4th April, 8th April, 2 P.M., one from W.A. Tait, Porto, and one from John Wilby, Lisbon, 8th April 1851. Tait's letter enclosed W.W.'s draft, on me at 20 months, finished 8th April 1851 for $1,183.00. $664.00 in favour of Coutinho and Lobo for my acceptance.

Monday, 30th June

Wrote to John Searle and Joseph Clark asking their leave to accept my Father's Draft.

Tuesday, 1st July

Received answers from Searle & Clark (on the letters I wrote them both acceding to my request) accepted the Draft. Closed and posted the following letters: to Liz No. 94, to Mrs. W. Wilby, enclosed to Liz for perusal (a few truths and a bit of my mind), one to my Father telling him I had accepted the Bill and one to W.A. Tait covering Bill accepted, sent with my Father's through (...illegible...), also in Tait's a letter to Coutinho and Lobo about the Bill.

Saturday, 5th July

Laidley went in the launch to bring cargo for Chinese Pereira, a half Portuguese and half Chinaman; lost my boat for me.

Sunday, 6th July

Lost the day in seeing after Pereira to look for the boat. António Dias turned up, had been working on board the *Oregon*, gets good wages.

Monday, 7th July

A boating trip.

Tuesday, 8th July

Fairy lost. Received from Packet Liz's Nos. 7 and 8 closed 20th April, Porto and 6th May 1851, and from George Searle 2nd May 1851.

Friday, 11th July

Captain Slater of the *Desire* arrived from Monterey, where he left his mate to bring the schooner up here. He brought me a letter from Mr. Whiteley dated 14th December 1850, acknowledging receipt of my letter.

Jim Stuart was hung today by the Committee, a well-merited punishment.

Sunday, 13th July

I attended service at the Marine Hospital where Reverend A. Williams officiated, the church being burnt down.

Monday, 14th July

Closed and posted my No. 95 to Liz, sent per Gregory's express per *Pacific* (steamer) also my petition to the Spanish Minister at Washington for the appointment of Spanish Consul enclosed in a letter to Thos. Stalker of New York and sent per same conveyance.

Tuesday, 15th July

Closed and posted per Packet, my No. 96 to Liz enclosed along with a letter to my Father in one to Uncle John. Also wrote to Aunt Elizabeth enclosed by Clark.

Sophy received on 26th October 1850 John's letter closed 13th July and sent via *Nicaragua*, per same steamer as mine which is lost.

Wednesday, 16th July

Desire entered, 202 days from Porto, last 7 from Monterey, came alongside next morning.

Sunday, 20th July

Went to church with Slater to the Presbyterian Church.

Monday, 21ˢᵗ July

Received Liz's No. 9 closed 13ᵗʰ May, has received my No. 85 closed 5ᵗʰ March 1851.

Tuesday, 22ⁿᵈ July

Alarm of fire in the evening.

Sunday, 27ᵗʰ July

Slater drowned about 3½ P.M. whilst sailing in the bay and with him the Captain of the *William* (an English ship), Mr. Mackolm of the same, Captain Ward of the *Robert Bruce* and four hands, Captain Crowell of the *Burmah*, the only survivor, was picked up much exhausted.

Monday, 28ᵗʰ

Went with Searle and the two mates of the *Desire* around Yerba Buena Island[126] to look for the bodies, but unsuccessful.

Friday, 1ˢᵗ August

Closed and posted my No. 97 to Liz (gave it to Searle to forward). Posted my letter closed 30ᵗʰ Valparaiso to Mr. Whiteley. Wrote to Mrs. George Henry Slater, care of Michael Duffield Slater, Brighton, to tell her of the death of her husband. All to go per *Oregon*.

Monday, 4ᵗʰ August

Received per Packet Liz's No. 10 dated 22ⁿᵈ May to 5ᵗʰ June 1851, had received (ere commencing her letter) my No. 86 closed 15ᵗʰ March. Rawes is very ill[127], my Father with Lavinia going to see him, also Mrs. Chaster expected up to keep Mrs. Rawes company. Mrs. Tait still at Figueira.

---

[126] Island in the centre of San Francisco Bay, originally Sea Bird Island now commonly known as Goat Island.
[127] James Rawes, husband of Mary Elizabeth Wilby, HEW's aunt, died in Porto on 13 July 1851.

Tuesday, 5ᵗʰ August

Spent the evening at Captain Simpton's (Harbour Master's) where Captain and Mrs. Gardiner are lodging; Miss Mary S. played the piano and we passed a pleasant evening.

Thursday, 7ᵗʰ August

Captain Tetherington hauled off his ship from alongside the *Gloucester* and we hauled the *Desire* into his berth.

(PAGE MISSING)

(…) for the horror Captain Crowell (the survivor) has of alluding to the accident as he told me there was fearful struggling to get clear of each other. The coffin closed and let down into grave No. 1261, Mackholm's grave, who was drowned same time, was buried in No. 1258, next but one to him, and the funeral service read by the Consul akin, we returned to town (Chaise hire for about 2 hours $15.00).

Sunday, 10ᵗʰ August

This morning's paper brings news of the *Urania* from Porto having been spoken per *Bengal* on August 2ⁿᵈ in Lat. 36.20 N. Long. 135 W. She is well up for the port and ought to be here soon. Was at Church morning and evening. Church embarrassed "2,000.00 wanted to pay parson's arrears; 10 persons present guaranteed to raise about $3,000.00 to build a temporary church. I subscribed $10.00 for the parson Reverend A. Williams.

Monday, 11ᵗʰ August

Zealous[128] arrived in 144 days. The *Zealous* from Lisbon consigned to us, arrived today flying her 2 white flags at the fore. I went with Searle on board, and got a ducking, the boat (a heavy sea on) gave a lurch and sent me slap over her gunwale, I seized the bench and held on till Searle who had already got on board, jumped down and hauled

---

[128] In *San Francisco Chronicle*: August 11: British Barque Zealous, Captain [*sic*] Wilson, 142 days from Lisbon. Wine, etc., to Searle, Wilby & Clark.

me in, but got well soaked and my watch full of water. Captain had gone to our office.

I went today also with the other witnesses to make affidavit at the Consul's of having identified Salter's body. On the 56th day of her voyage, the *Zealous* was in latitude 50 south in the Pacific! *Witchcraft* is in 62 days from Rio! 102 from N.Y

Tuesday, 12th August

Brig *Enigma* (Portuguese) from Lisbon consigned to Wynn, came in this morning, 230 days passage. *Zealous* come up but did not get alongside.

Friday, 15th August

Closed and delivered to Searle to post my No. 98 to Liz.

We have for some months had very fine weather but strong winds, and the heat has been greater indicating the early approach of rain. The rainy season has long since set in, in Panama, where the roads are almost impassable.

Sunday, 17th August

The first rain fell today, softly, very close, Southerly wind. *Urania* arrived, having sailed from Porto 14th March, in 153 days.

Wednesday, 20th August

Packet in but no letters for me. Jim Garland says in his letter to John that Liz's letter would arrive in Lisbon the day after the Packet left. Mackenzie and Wittaker, two criminals in the hands of the Vigilance Committee and by them sentenced to be hung this morning, were early this morning rescued from them by the Sheriff or Marshall, by an express order of the Governor McDugal.

Also it is said there was treachery on the part of those who were on guard at the time; it is said the Committee have put their guard in irons. A large meeting was held to consider as to measures to be adopted by the Committee with regard to the criminals. They have circulated a report that they will do nothing further in the case as they will not act against the law, but I presume it is to cover their intention of recapturing the prisoners.

Sunday, 24ᵗʰ August

On returning from Church, I heard the Vigilance Bell tapping and seeing everyone running in the direction of the Rooms, went ashore and got there about two minutes after Mackenzie and Wittaker had been hung up from the two gable ends of the Committee Rooms. A body of sixteen men had been appointed to take these two criminals out of jail and hung them, accordingly they went there, got them out, put them into a carriage and 17 minutes after had them hanging out of their windows. Nearly everyone in town went to see them hanging and general approbation was expressed by all.

Monday, 1ˢᵗ September

Closed my No. 99 to Liz and gave it to John to post. Also closed a letter to [*sic.*] Sarah Alice and Louisa, thanking them for their presents. Clark enclosed it for me in one of his letters.

Sunday, 7ᵗʰ September

First rain. Last night we had the first heavy rain of the season and it rained pretty hard; our decks were very leaky and the water came into our berths in streams. I had to keep pots and pans all over my bed and even so, could get no sleep. This morning when I got up, found all my clothes wet and had to stay on board all day to get them dried.

Monday, 8ᵗʰ September

A beautiful day, *verão de São Martinho*[129] has begun. Received per Packet the following letters: one from W. Wilby dated Vizella 5ᵗʰ June 1851, had received mine of 19ᵗʰ January 1851, informs me of Uncle

---

[129] Unseasonably warm autumn weather, attributed in Portugal to St. Martin. The US equivalent is an Indian Summer.

Sam[130]'s death and of Rawes' serious illness. A letter from Mrs. Rawes dated Candal[131] 25th June 1851, also about Rawes' illness. Also received Liz's No. 11 in which she acknowledges receipt of my Nos. 87 and 88, the latter received on the 16th June only 2 months and 30 hours old, the former she received on the 9th June.

Saturday, 13th September

The two last nights we have been fishing with the casting nets and caught plenty of fish, some very large, but tonight I am better employed writing for the Packet. This day brings with it reminiscences of 5 years ago which almost unfit me for writing[132] After sitting up till midnight and getting on but slowly with my letter, I wrote some lines for a certain lady's album and when I turned in, it was past 1 A.M. of the 14th.

Sunday, 14th September

Searle went out fishing this morning and caught with a line, lots of rock cod off Rincorn Point. I only just got up in time to go to church after which I walked out to the Presidio to the tent of Cornelius Johnston, or Johnson, where I expected to hear news of Edward Rumsey[133], no one in tent, left a note requesting information relative to him, be left at our office. I walked out there in an hour and five minutes and back in 1 hour and 20 min. I found in the tent, a book with Rumsey's name in it.

---

[130] Samuel Wilby 1791-1851, married to Margaret Binns, brother to William Wilby.

[131] Parish of Vila Nova de Gaia, above the Port Wine lodges, on the South bank of the River Douro.

[132] *Viz.* HEW's diary entries of 1846 in which he details a serious pulmonary illness in Porto.

[133] Dr. Edward Rumsey (1790-1855) came from Amersham, Bucks, to set up in private practice at Porto in 1816. He married Catherine Cock who bore him eight children, most of whom married English and Portuguese Port Wine families and stayed in Porto.

Foot Race run at the mission by Guildersleeve (to be 10 Miles in less than 1 hour) in consequence of a strong wind he took 63 minutes and 5 seconds to run it.[134]

Monday, 15th September

Closed two long letters, one to Liz No. 100 enclosing in it an extract of pay of my letter to my Dad relative to her and a few lines written on Saturday night 13th instant. The other letter was to my Father. I closed the two letters in an envelope to Spencer and Budden of London and took them to the post myself and prepaid it. 57 cents.

Friday, 19th September

Clark did not make his appearance at office till midday having been drunk the night before and slept, he said, on the floor at Sam Price's! Last night he lost $30.00 at cards and came today to get it off Searle to pay his debt. I refused it having no cash to spare as we are hard up!

Clark is beyond recovery. When a lesson like the last will not mend him and promises like his last breaks, it is a bad case; he is bound to ruin. Persons are often, when called on for small amounts owing to the house, answering "Will I settle with Clark as he is owing me money". When he is taxed with it, "yes, put it to my account!" How much he may owe me besides, I do not know.

---

[134] «The great Foot Race for $1,000, being a match against time, ten miles to be done within the hour (…) and there appeared John Gildersleeve, B.F. Gorin, and -- Kearney. Gildersleeve was dressed with a tight shirt, blue silk knee breeches, bare legs below the knee, and thin-soled shoes. The other two, who appeared to be amateurs, had not paid particular attention to their style of dress, and appeared to have entered more for sport than anything else. There was but very little betting. The wind was blowing a perfect gale from the Northwest, and it was very generally conceded that, under the circumstances, the 10 miles could not be done within the hour. (…) By the hour watch, the time was made in sixty-three minutes, thirty seconds. Gildersleeve, as will be seen by the time, kept up a very regular pace, and was very fresh, when he came in.» In: *Daily Alta California*, September 15, 1851

Very calm night, went fishing with net and caught lots of fish.

Saturday, 20ᵗʰ September
Packet in, letters for me, one from John Wilby, closed 17ᵗʰ June 1851 and No. 12 from Liz closed 15ᵗʰ July. Rawes not expected to live many hours; on the 25ᵗʰ June, she received my No. 89 closed 1ˢᵗ May, 54 days old only! Discharged our 3 workmen, left only with Laidley and ourselves.

Omitted from Friday, 19ᵗʰ September
Spent the first evening in California as I should wish to do, occasionally, and as I was accustomed to do at home. Spent it at Captain Simpton's (Harbour Master) where Mrs. Gardiner is staying. They have a very comfortable house, large drawing room with fireplace, carpet, piano and very comfortable.

Miss Mary Ellen Simpton played the Piano and sang. She is a lively intelligent girl, plays well and brought back to my mind the good old times at home. I danced two quadrilles with Mrs. Gardiner and Mrs. Wilson. Other two young Ladies there besides the above and Mrs. Simpton, also two officers from the M.B. of W. *Daffney* waltzing Polka. Ducks and wild geese begin to appear, but few yet.

Sunday, 21ˢᵗ September
Went to the Episcopal Church Trinity, but Vermheyer preached there and I could not understand half he said.

Tuesday, 23ʳᵈ September
Ferreira, ex-mate of *Emma* came to offer me a partnership in a sloop to go into the trade of furnishing provisions and vegetables from the contracosta[135] for ships etc. I referred the offer to Searle, who turned up his nose at it and refused to enter into it, therefore here I am like a thirsty horse, tied short up over a river unable to drink.

---

[135] The coast on the other side, i.e., the other side of the bay.

That trade could pay better than anything sold and gives ready cash at once, the profits are tangible within a day or two; here goes another link to the chain that is clasped to my legs in the form of two partners. The man who enters into partnership and bound to keep to it for a certain time ought to be confined in a lunatic asylum for a fool. Cleared the *Desire* and saw her safe on her way to Valparaiso with casks of our wines on board, consigned to Watson, Thompson and Co. there.

Wednesday, 29th September

Mr. Mace slept on board of our ship. She is back from Sacramento disheartened with things in general. He says he ate a piece of an extraordinary sized watermelon, 76 lbs. Weight.

Monday, 29th September

Cook Oscar left us.

Tuesday, 30th September

Shipped on a new cook, John Wilson, at $60.00. Laidley went to the mines via Sacramento Street; rent $150.00 per month for the two stores. Closed for the mail my two letters, one to Mrs. W. Wilby and one No. 101 to Eliza, both were by Searle enclosed in a business letter to John Wilby through Prescotts.

Saturday, 4th October

Let ½ of the new store for $75.00 to Scott McFarlane's son-in-law.

Sunday, 5th October

At church in morning, new church on old lot in Stockton Street, ready to be opened next Sunday. Introduced at the store to Mrs. Scott McFarlane's daughter.

Monday, 6th October

Received from Packet, 3 letters, two from W. Wilby dated *viz*. 3rd July and Candal 28th July 1851 and Liz's No. 13 closed July. The last letter from Father contained news of Rawes' death at noon 13th July

1851. Spencer and Budden had not handed over the balance of gold dust, but Father had got $48.00 off Tait *adiantado*[136], on account of the $30.00 I remitted through them. Liz received my No. (...) closed 12th May 1851 on the 16th July 1851, enclosed in her letter came court (...illegible...) from Buarcos [?].

$$\mathcal{C} \infty_{\gamma} \approx \mathcal{D}$$

---

[136] In advance

TO THE GOLD MINES

Friday, 10th October

Wrote to Liz my No. 2, only just a few lines to say that I am going today to the mines, and left it for John to forward.

* * *

At 5 P.M. started for Sacramento City in the *Senator* and got there at 6 next morning, having been stuck in the mud for better than 2 hours. 150 miles in 13 hours from wharf to wharf, fare $1.00, touching at Benicia.

Sacramento City. Saturday, 11th October

Arrived here at 6 A.M., breakfasted at the Crescent City Hotel for 75 cents then took the stage coach through Cossumes, Dayles Ranch, Arkansaw diggings, Rancheria Amadore, Willow Springs, Sutter Creek, and Dry Town to Jackson. 65 miles in 7 hours, stoppages included; fare $8.00. Dinner on the road, splendid, $1.00.

The country this side of Willow Spring is a vast dreary plain, without a tree or shrub to be seen, except as that place is approached, when fine oak trees and shrubs; from that up the country is very hilly and gradually more picturesque, but no pasturage.

After arriving at Jackson, I went out to look for Pereira (mate of the *Emma*). I found him with five other Portuguese, encamped on China Hill amongst lots of Chinamen. I then returned to Iowa House, kept by Mr. and Mrs. Tait, Americans who came over the plains.

Sunday, 12th October

Spent the greater part of the day in walking about and seeing the place. A part of the day I spent alone up one of the beautiful ravines. It was during the heat of the day and under the shade of the trees, I laid down and admired the beauties of Nature. When I cannot choose my company I like at least to be alone.

It is pretty to see all the families clean and decent sitting outside their tents on a Sunday, most of the men brush up and come into town, some to gamble, others to lounge about or get the news from their friends.

Jackson Mines. Monday, 13th October

Went about watching the miners. All the dry bed of the river is dug in sundry claims varying from two to 15 feet deep; many of these pits having been abandoned by those who dug them, have been taken up by others and coyote, and these coyotes have paid well.

There are thousands of buckets of earth thrown up there, ready to wash as soon as the rain comes, but at present the richest diggings will scarcely pay, for the water is so scarce that when the earth is to be carried to it one half of the time is lost in going backwards and forwards. Few of the miners are making their expenses new, but no doubt 16 to 20 Dollars each may be made as soon as rain comes.

The Portuguese have spent upwards of $200.00 and not got over $8.00 of gold but they do not work. Part of them have a good sprinkling of Chinese blood in them and those half breeds are not worth their salt "*Faz muito calor*"[137] from morning till night; besides they do not have the least idea of mining. Picked flowers to send home.

Tuesday, 14th October

Agreed with Ferreira to go shares in mining, so went to work with him and opened a new mine in the riverbed. We worked hard and from all appearances we had made a good selection.

Wednesday, 15th October

Having got to the bedrock, we carried a few bags of earth from the top of the rock and washed it, taking out about $2.00 worth of gold; good beginning. Tired at night. Wrote to Searle to tell him that I could sell a little wine if I had samples and requesting him to send me word to Sacramento if I am wanted.

---

[137] It's far too hot!

Thursday, 16th October

Worked away at our mine and did pretty well. I marked out all the ground round us in claims and set all the other Portuguese at working in them. In the evening news was received of very rich diggings being found in Indian Gulch and resolved to go a prospecting tomorrow.

Friday, 17th October

Prospected all over the neighbouring gulches, brought down two bags of dirt and washed them; it would not pay to carry it so far as we did, near two miles, but to wash it where we did it, when the rain comes, a man may make above $16.00 per day.

Same day saw a Mexican pan out two lumps of gold, one the size and shape of a pigeon's egg, and the other the size of a cherry. Two Frenchmen in the next mine to ours panned out in about a quarter of an hour, 3oz. of gold.

❧❧❧

The last pages of the original Diary were torn or cut out – so we do not know the rest of the story. However, Henry Edward's son George, in a 1934 conversation with the Vancouver City Achivist, makes a comment that may shed some light as to what then happened:

> "On arrival in San Francisco they started off for the goldfields, struck nothing, and returned to San Francisco. The crew on being paid off, went to the mines so the ship was used as floating warehouse; there were a whole row of ships similarly employed; they were anchored in a portion of the bay which has since been filled in, and the site is now several blocks inland from the waterfront. It was safer to store goods in this way than in the wooden shacks along the shore when they were liable to destruction by fire." [138]

---

[138] Conversation between Major J. S. Matthews, City Archivist, Vancouver and Mr. George Wilby of the composing room staff, *The Sun*, Vancouver, October 10, 1934. From the City of Vancouver Archives.

SAN FRANCISCO DIRECTORY
1852 – 53
EMBRACING A GENERAL DIRECTORY OF CITIZENS

Wilby H E. Vice Con Portugal, 71 Jack
Wilby H E. imp & com mer, 71 Jack

Gibbs & Bo., importers and commission merchants, Granite Block, California
Gibbs, C.V.S. 64 California, h Broadway, 3 doors ab Stockton
Gibbs, Chas. E. 64 California, h Broadway, 3 doors ab Stockton
Gibbs, F.A. clerk, 64 California, h Broadway, 3 doors ab Stockton
Gibbs, E.B. clerk, 64 California, h Braodway, 3 doors ab Stockton
Gibb, Daniel & Co., merchants, 122 Commercial

Other San Francisco City Directory 1852:

Searle & Wynn, commission merchants, 127 California
Searle, John, Portuguese consul, 127 California

Gibb, Daniel, merchant, Central wharf
Gibbs, C. V. S., of Dunbar & Gibbs, c Sansome and Wash
Gibbs, C. V. S., of Dunbar & Gibbs, merchant, c Wash and Virg
Gibbs, George, trader, Stockton b P and J
Gibbs, John S., at J. Cowell & Co., c Jackson and San

PART 5

REPORT ON CALIFORNIA FROM JOHN SEARLE TO THE PORTUGUESE MINISTER FOR FOREIGN AFFAIRS
1851[139]
Marked Received 4 Feb 1851

**CONSULATE OF PORTUGAL
SAN FRANCISCO, CALIFORNIA**

Lisbon, 17 January 1851

To His Excellency the Count of Tojal
Minister and Secretary of State for Foreign Affairs

Your Excellency,

Pursuant to my duty, I respectfully address Your Excellency to report on the state of the Country which is being so talked about in Europe and which has created a considerable amount of commercial movement.

---

[139] Translated from the Portuguese by Magdalena Gorrell Guimaraens

113

Permit me, Your Excellency, that before I give you the due report, I inform Your Excellency that, having sailed from Portugal in the month of November of 1849, I rounded Cape Horn in February 1850 and docked in San Francisco, California, on the 13ᵗʰ of June. As soon as I disembarked, I presented my credentials to the Authorities of the United States of America who immediately acknowledged me as Consul for Portugal.

I did not inform His Majesty's Government of my arrival, nor did I write afterwards, because I lacked the time to enable me to obtain particulars of this infant country. Furthermore, after three months and having resolved to travel to Europe to deal with my affairs, I felt that I could myself convey information that might be of interest to His Majesty's Government and to Portuguese commerce.

Prior to my departure, I appointed Mr. Henrique Eduardo[140] Wilby as pro-tem Vice Consul for Portugal in San Francisco in order to ensure that there is no lack of services rendered during my absence, which shall be limited as I plan to return next April.

I trust that Your Excellency, attending the extraordinary circumstances that motivated my departure and the lack of regular communications with Portugal, will excuse my having absented myself without leave and respectfully deign to endorse the steps that I was obliged to take, for purposes of regularising the affairs of the Consulate.

There are three sea ports: San Francisco, Monte Rei and San Diego; the first is the one that offers greater commercial advantages as it is more comfortable and more convenient for trading with the mines, located in two cities – Sacramento and Stockton, and in many small towns and hamlets.

The Port of San Francisco, which is 25 miles long and 14 miles wide, is perfectly sheltered from all sides and the entrance is easy and good.

The Seat of the Government is located in the City of San José, a distance of 30 miles inland from San Francisco. The Laws are the

---

[140] Portuguese form for Henry Edward

same as those of the United States of America, the cities and towns are totally calm and there is more law and order in the mines than one would expect.

The rivers are large and they offer communications with all the mining sites by means of sail and steam boats of which there are a great many.

There is only one Customs Office and this is established in San Francisco and is currently administered with great diligence. The excise duties are the same as for the United States of America, everything being taxed *ad valorem*.

The Port Charges for Portuguese ships are as follows: Piloting, 7.360 *milreis*[141] per draught foot, half that amount if the ship does not take on a Pilot. Health Visit, 23.000 *milreis*. Captain of the Port, 9.200 *milreis*. Maritime Hospital, for each sailor or steerage passenger, 1.840 *milreis*, Captain and first class passengers, 2.760 *milreis* each. Piloting from one side of the harbour to another, 46.000 *milreis*, but one is not obliged to take on a Pilot.

The mines continue to produce large amounts of gold. Four million five hundred thousand *reis* worth of gold is exported monthly by steam ship to New York and London, free of duty for everyone, although foreign miners pay a monthly tax of 20 *Patacas* or 18.400 *milreis*, which in all probability will soon end.

It is impossible to know exactly how many inhabitants there are in California, although the population is calculated at around 300,000, almost all of whom are men; women and children currently represent about 2% of the total.

As to imports from Portugal, so far these goods have been very limited although there is a demand for wine and other products from this kingdom, principally those which are currently exported to the United States; consumption should rise with the increase in population.

---

[141] Old Portuguese currency. 1 *Milrei* = *1,000 reis*. Also described as a *conto de reis*. With the fall of the Monarchy, the *reis* was replaced by the *Escudo*. A *Conto* was equivalent to 1,000 escudos, the official currency until the adoption of the euro.

There is only one export – gold.

All sales and purchases are transacted cash in hand, payments are made in gold and silver coins from every country and in gold dust at the rate of 16 *patacas*[142] per ounce. The London Exchange rate is 48 pence per *pataca* for Sight Bills at 90 days. Considering the Lisbon-London exchange rate at an average of 54 pence per *milreis*, the equivalent value in San Francisco is 1 *pataca* = 888 Portuguese *reis*.

Agriculture is in its infancy and it will not increase much as long as wages continue to be so exhorbitantly high – a worker earns 5 *patacas* or 4.500 *milreis* per day.

God preserve Your Excellency.

/s/

João Searle[143]
Consul of Portugal in California

---

[142] Another old Portuguese currency, originally from Macao but introduced by custom to Portugal. The expression "Arvore das Patacas", or money tree, referring to the great fortunes that were made from trade with Macao and the Far East in the 16th century, is still used today when stating that such-and-such a venture is not a get-rich-quick scheme.

[143] John Searle signed the letter with the Portuguese form of his name: João.

+ + + + + +
# PART 6
+ + + + + +

A VOYAGE AND TWO MARRIAGES

When Henry Edward sailed from Porto on 22 October 1849, he was engaged to Eliza Antoinette Searle and John Searle was engaged to Sophia Laidley. The girls promised to follow their beaus to San Francisco and so they did. On March 25th, 1853, two young ladies and a servant left Porto in charge of an English gentleman, Dr. Jelly, on their way to San Francisco via the Isthmus of Panama, which they crossed most of the way on the backs of mules over the rocky trails. From Panama, they boarded a steamship for San Francisco where their fiancés were to meet them.[144]

The wedding was memorialized June 29, 1853, by Captain W.H. Hudson, U. S. Navy Commander, SS *Panama*, in his report on the voyage:

---

[144] A much earlier transcriber of the diary said that both girls were aged 17 when their fiancés left for California. This is very clearly incorrect as Eliza's death certificate states she was over 95 years of age when she died in 1922 and gives her birthdate as 16 March 1826 in Porto which would make her a much more credible 23 years old. This mistake was originally made in a newspaper article of March 8 1951 (*Victoria Daily Colonist*) and erroneously repeated elsewhere.

MARRIED

On board the U.S.M. steamer Panama, in the harbour of San Francisco, on Wednesday, the 29th inst., by the Rev. Mr. Wyatt, of Trinity Church, **JOHN SEARLE, Esq., Her Most Faithful Majesty's Consul,** to **MISS SOPHIA LAIDLEY,** of Figueira, Portugal, and **MR. HENRY E. WILBY to MISS ELIZA SEARLE**, both of Porto, Portugal.[145]

❧

---

[145] As published in the *Daily Alta California,* June 30 1853.

FROM LIVERPOOL TO SAN FRANCISCO IN 1853
BY ELIZA ANTOINETTE SEARLE WILBY

**Extracted from an article entitled "Pioneer Women of B.C."
published in the June 11 1909 issue of
the *Victoria Daily Colonist.***

«Early in May 1853, a party of four of us sailed from Liverpool on the boat *S.S. Africa* on our way to California. The accommodation and fare were splendid, and the vessel was not overcrowded with passengers, which made it pleasant, and we had a safe passage of twelve days to New York, which at that time was considered a good medium passage.

When we arrived at New York we were disappointed to find that the steamer which was to leave next day for Aspinwall and by which we hoped to have gone, had all the berths engaged with the exception of one or two, and as we needed four we had to wait for the next boat, which would oblige us to remain in New York over a week. We put up at the Astor house. We were very comfortable, and as we had friends in the city the time passed quite pleasantly until the time for the next boat to leave, when we sailed on the *Crescent City*, and after a nine-days' voyage reached Aspenwall. As it was late in the evening when we arrived, we remained on board all night.

In the morning we took the train as far as it went, which I think, was about twenty-five miles. We went very slowly which gave us the opportunity of seeing the beautiful trees through which we passed. When we left the train we had to travel in a boat, on a lake or river, I am not sure which, pulled by scantily clothed natives who took it very easy, not inclined to hurry, sometimes stopping to chat with their friends whom they saw on the banks of the river, so that it was getting nearly dark when we reached the placed where we were to stop all night. I think the place was called Gorgona. The hotel certainly was a very primitive affair; the boards forming the partition in our room were so shrunk that we could see into the next room.

In the morning we started on mules for the rest of our journey to Panama. The mules had men's saddles, as they told us the roads were so bad it was safer for the women to ride on men's saddles. However, my sister-in-law and I objected, and got them to change the saddles on our mules, as we assured them we were used to riding on horseback. Certainly the roads were ..... to compare with these. In some places it was going down steep stairs with walls of rock on either side, so that if the mule fell there was no room to get away, but you would have to roll right down with the mule. Then there was what they called the Corduroy road, which were trees cut down and laid across swamps. Some of the passengers road over them but we preferred walking, although by so doing our skirts got dreadfully muddy.

The day we were on the train was a lovely one but when we were on the mules we had some very heavy showers, after which the sun would come out very hot, and as we were through we felt like being in a steam bath.

It was nearly dark when we reached Panama, soaking wet, and as our luggage had not come on as quickly as we did, we had to go to a ready made shop to get outfits, and we were disappointed to learn that the steamship company had altered the time of their boats sailing, and that instead of one a week there would only be one in two weeks, which would oblige us to remain more than a week in Panama. This was a serious affair, for it is such an unhealthy place. Some of the passengers wrote a petition to the company requesting that they should start a steamer as soon as possible to take them on. I think we signed it with the result that they got the steamer *Panama* ready, and we sailed on Sunday afternoon for San Francisco, which place we reached in sixteen days.

On our way we called at Acapulco, where we left two bodies of passengers who had died on the way. There were three deaths during the voyage. The last was an old lady who was coming to her sons in San Francisco, who had the sorrow of only finding her body when they came to meet her, she having died the night before reaching the city.

Two of our party got the Panama fever[146], but were mercifully restored to health.

In those days when steamers were often crowded, deaths were frequent from Panama fever. Travelling in those days was very different from what it is now.»

---

[146] Ague: Malarial or intermittent fever characterized by paroxysms (stages of chills, fever, and sweating at regularly recurring times) and followed by an interval or intermission of varying duration. Popularly, the disease was known as "fever and ague," "chill fever," "the shakes," and by names expressive of the locality in which it was prevalent, such as, "swamp fever" (in Louisiana), "Panama fever," and "Chagres fever."

MRS. HY. EDWARD WILBY
BY EDGAR FAWCETT

This article is transcribed verbatim from the original found in the BC Provincial Archives. Edgar Fawcett was a pioneer to Victoria and wrote many newspaper articles on Old Victoria and notable residents. No date is given but as he mentions Eliza's recent death – it must be Feb. 1922.

Another link connected with the past of Old VICTORIA, has gone to her reward in the person of Mrs. Henry Wilby whom I have long known, with her husband since 1859 (he deceased many years). I used to meet her often, on her way to or from the hospitals, on her mission of mercy. And she has now gone to receive her reward. The family arrived in Victoria the same year as our family 1859, and from San Francisco, and strange to say went to live on the same street, so we were friends from the first. The following account of the families life, and, travels in the early days of San Francisco, are give concisely by one of the family and I have added what I know of one "who went about doing good." The hospitals knew her, and that right well, until the weight of years compelled her with regret to say good bye to them, but not before she had pointed many a skeptic or wayward one into the right path. I met her often and conversed with her on her success, and she admitted that she was satisfied with the result. She leaves us, only 2 months short of 96 years of age. Requiscat in pace.

⌐   ⌐   ⌐

Henry Edward Wilby was born in Porto, Portugal, May 4th, 1823. When a boy he was sent to Yorkshire to school, returning to Portugal he went with his father to live in Lisbon where he entered his fathers office as clerk. Later he was employed by the Portuguese government to superintend some road building, through the country. Mr. Wilby spoke and wrote the Portuguese language quite fluently.

Returning again to Porto in the year 1849 he formed a partnership (Searle, Wilby & Clark) and purchased a small sailing vessel, named the Bella Pernambucana (Captain Bannister) afterwards master of one of the Hudson Bay Co.'s ships from England to Victoria.

The Bella Pernambucana was partly filled with goods, which the partners purchased, as speculation, and partly with goods on consignment, to be sold when the vessel arrived at San Francisco, which was her destination.

The vessel sailed in October 1849 from Porto and arrived at San Francisco in June 1850. On her way, she called at Lisbon, Brazil, and Valparaiso, picking up any cargo that was offered. The details of this long voyage would make too long a story. They encountered dreadful storms off Cape Horn, which carried away the hen coops and pig stys. At one time the main yard arm dragged in the sea for some time and all on board thought the ship would never right herself again.

On arriving in San Francisco, the vessel was dismantled and anchored in the bay with dozens of others, as a storeship, as people stored goods on vessels in case of fire on shore. While in San Francisco, Mr. Wilby was for some time Portuguese Consul, there were in those days a great number of Portuguese people in San Francisco.

Mrs. H.E. Wilby, at the age of 17 went to Porto, and met her future husband. March 25th, 1853 she left Portugal with a Miss Laidlee who was like herself, journing to San Francisco to be married to Mr. Searle of the firm of Searle, Wilby & Clark. These two young ladies left Portugal March 25th, 1853 and arrived at San Francisco June 29th. They traveled in charge of an English gentleman named Dr. Jelly. They crossed the Isthmas of Panama, riding most of the way on the backs of mules, over the rocky trails. At Panama they took passage on a steamer (named the Panama) to San Francisco.

On arriving, the two young ladies were married on board the *Panama*, to their respective husbands by Rev. Dr. Wyatt, Episcopal minister.

Mr. and Mrs. Wilby went to live on board their storeship, (as many whole families were doing.) They lived on board for about six months, then owing to the continual rolling of the vessel they were compelled to reside on shore renting a 5 room house unfurnished for $75.00 per month.

In 1859 Mr. and Mrs. Wilby with their three children left San Francisco for Victoria, on board the Streamer *Otter* (Captain Mouatt). The voyage took just 10 days and 16 hours. On arriving in Victoria they went to live in a small house on Broughton Street (then Kane St.) The number of the house 850, and still stands, and is occupied.

In 1863 Mr. and Mrs. Wilby went to live in Esquimalt. Mr. Wilby conducted the Post Office in Esquimalt for some years and also carried the mails between Victoria and Esquimalt.

PART 7

EPILOGUE

Like many other families, Henry Edward and Eliza Wilby lived on board their storeship for about six months until the continuous rolling of the ship forced them to move ashore. They rented a 5-room house where three of their eight children, MaryAnne, Edward and Alice, were born. The Wilbys remained in San Francisco for another 6 years until Henry Edward, ever the adventurer, resolved to move his family and seek his future in another new territory, Canada. In 1859, Henry Edward, Eliza and their young family travelled to the tiny port of Esquimault, Victoria, British Columbia on the steamer *Otter*, a voyage that took them 10 days and half.

Henry Edward and Eliza's first home in Victoria was a modest dwelling on Kane Street, on the outskirts of the town. Some time later, Henry Edward built an elegant family home that still stands on Yates Street, in one of the more fashionable neighbourhoods of Victoria. Five more children were born in Canada to Henry Edward and Eliza: Annie, William, Mary Elizabeth, George and James and these in turn produced 29 grandchildren.

In Victoria, Henry Edward engaged in different ventures including Postmaster, commission sales, opening a general store and as acting Vice Consul for Portugal. One of Henry Edward's more pioneering initiatives was creating an express mail service from Victoria to Esquimault, at that time the port of call for the San Francisco steamer.

On 9 February 1888, whilst on a visit to his family in Porto, where he was born, Henry Edward, aged 65, died from pneumonia that he contracted whilst travelling down from the Port Wine vineyards in the Alto Douro Winemaking Region. He is buried next to his father in St. James Church British Cemetery in Porto. Eliza passed away peacefully in Victoria on February 7th 1922, just 2 months short of her 96th birthday.

ELIZA ANTOINETTE (SEARLE) WILBY
1826 Porto, Portugal
1922 Victoria BC, Canada

HENRY EDWARD WILBY
1823 – 1888 Porto, Portugal

JOHN AND SOPHIA (LAIDLEY) SEARLE and Family

John and Sofia Searle never left California where they settled down to the life of prosperous merchants and active members of the community. John died in San Francisco in 1879 at the age of 61 years. Sofia died in San Benito California twenty-six years later, in 1905, aged 87 years.

POSTSCRIPT

Who was CLARK, Henry Edward and John's partner in Searle, Wilby & Clark?

Henry Edward never referred to his partner Clark by his first name, not even when, in his Diary, he was especially annoyed with him. It would appear that unlike John Searle, they were not really friends, perhaps just fellow investors in the venture. He is identified in the beginning as "Joseph" Clark, although this is an assumption based on a stray mention in some family papers. Current research into official Portuguese ship registration documents for the early 1840s may confirm his name as one of the ship's owners, but this information is providing extremely difficult to find.

Try as I might, I have been unable to find any reference to a "Clark" in the Porto British community at the time of the voyage. I searched Factory House Records, St. James Church Records, invaluable sources such as Sellar's *Oporto Old and New*, the community geneological bible, to no avail. It occurs to me that Clark was not a resident of Porto or Lisbon, but that he was an occasional visitor to Porto, possibly related to Patrick Clark, a Scotsman who had developed a ground-breaking cotton thread for use with textiles that was being acquired like wildfire all over the world. At the time of the Journey, two Scottish companies were sending family members worldwide as selling agents. These companies, Coats and Clark merged in 1896. A member of the Clark family would most likely be a frequent visitor to Porto and would have close commercial ties with local British textile merchants shipping agent and therefore happy to invest in a new venture.

The Family History. Marked discrepancies between Edgar Fawcett's article and some proven facts simply show how often-repeated family stories can unwittingly distort what actually happened. A notable example of this is that William Wilby never lived in Lisbon – the Laidley family did. Also, there is the oft repeated and rather "romantic" story that Henry Edward died from a fall on board ship. Whilst excerpts from his journals as a young man, together with his comments on his health during the voyage, would indicate that he was perhaps not the most robust of people and somewhat prone to affictions of the lungs, there is no question that the cause of his death in Porto was certified as pneumonia. Presumably, he fell ill when travelling back on horseback from the Alto Douro vineyards in wet weather. Yet another example of how important it is to ensure the correct transcription and recording of family history.

I dedicated several years of genealogical research into the Wilby and Guimaraens families and their Yorkshire roots and after many connections and leads thanks to Yorksgen, a Rootsweb Gen Site, now defunct. Although my husband Bruce had frequently visited Vancouver on business and asked about the Wilby family, we were unable to establish any connection with the Canadian Wilbys until I was contacted, via Internet, by John Wilby, one of Henry Edward's descendants.

Thanks to this newfound connection, I was able to add to the extensive, detailed genealogical record I had already built of the descendants of William Wilby, of Hartshead, Yorkshire, in Yorkshire, Vancouver, Portugal and Australia. John Wilby's contribution, as well as the copy of Henry Edward's Diary, together with new, Canadian, genealogical research, provided the impetus for a first trans-continental and trans-oceanic family reunion in Vancouver in 2000. This was followed in 2002 when over twenty of Henry Edward and Eliza's descendants travelled from Vancouver to join other Wilby descendants at a Family Reunion in Porto.

This event was celebrated with a small ceremony in honour of *O Senhor do Chalet,* Henry Edward's father William, as the Mayor of Vizela unveiled a bronze plaque set in a large boulder next to the Roman bridge, below where his house had stood. Henry Edward's descendants planted a Douglas Fir sapling they had brought with them from Victoria.

With this Diary, I have accompanied Henry Edward from his birthplace in Portugal to San Francisco on this incredible journey, leading up to his marriage to Eliza Antoinette. After they left California and settled in British Columbia with their children, he became a succesful merchant, a community leader and a notable pioneer of Vancouver. It is now up to one of his many descendants to tell the fascinating story of the Wilby Family in Canada.

www.ingramcontent.com/pod-product-compliance
Lightning Source LLC
Chambersburg PA
CBHW060304050426
42448CB00009B/1745